The Anxiety Workbook

The Anxiety Workbook

A 7-WEEK PLAN
to Overcome Anxiety, Stop Worrying, and End Panic

Arlin Cuncic, MA

Foreword by Seth J. Gillihan, PhD

ALTHEA
PRESS

CONTENTS

FOREWORD

"I feel like I'm fighting this battle every minute of every day."

It was my first time meeting Susan, who was feeling crushed under the weight of panic and worry. Her world had shrunk as she gave up activities that made her anxious, and yet her fears only grew. With every step of retreat she felt more demoralized. Susan's experience will resonate with millions of men and women in the United States. Anxiety disorders are the most common psychiatric diagnoses, affecting as many as one in three adults at some point in their lifetime, according to a 2015 study published in *Dialogues in Clinical Neuroscience.*

I've worked as a clinical psychologist for 15 years, and I've seen just how powerful the grip of anxiety can be. And countless times I've witnessed how courage, coupled with the right techniques, can break that grip. Much of what I learned about treating anxiety came from my time on the faculty at the University of Pennsylvania. I had just completed my PhD and wanted to work with Dr. Edna Foa, a giant in the field of anxiety treatment. She and her colleagues at Penn's Center for the Treatment and Study of Anxiety had developed some of the most effective cognitive behavioral therapy (CBT) programs for anxiety. During the years I collaborated with Dr. Foa, I came to recognize three powerful principles of effective anxiety treatment.

First, a compelling "why" helps us face our fears. Maybe the anxiety is hurting our closest relationships or getting in the way of our life's work. Another reason could be that we've decided our world is starting to feel like a prison cell and have resolved to gain our freedom—whatever it takes. Using CBT to treat anxiety is hard work and remembering why we're doing it can sustain our efforts.

I also learned that we can rewire our brain simply by facing our fears. When we confront our anxieties, they become more manageable—not all at once, but gradually and with repeated practice. Our confidence grows as we start to push back on our fears, helping us face even bigger challenges.

And finally, I saw the crucial role of acceptance in mastering our anxiety and living with greater ease. We can connect with our basic sanity as we stop resisting reality—the reality that life is inherently uncertain, that pain at times is inevitable, and that a certain degree of anxiety is unavoidable. And we find that despite pain, despite uncertainty, despite unexpected challenges, we can create a life of deep meaning and purpose.

I learned these things not only as a researcher and therapist. I have personally benefited countless times from the principles of CBT. I've experienced firsthand how the breath can calm an agitated nervous system, how worries diminish when I stop feeding them, and that I can refuse to let panic attacks limit what I do. Thus I feel a deeply personal passion for bringing effective treatment to those who need it, a passion born from my intimate understanding of anxiety and its treatment.

Arlin Cuncic shares my passion and it shines through in this book. Her passion is coupled with expertise as she presents the latest and best-tested approaches for managing anxiety. For years Arlin has shown her commitment to improving the lives of those with debilitating anxiety. She has been at the helm at Verywell.com, providing ready-to-use information for those who are struggling. Now she has pulled together the most important elements of effective treatment and crafted them into a 7-week self-guided program.

You have a rich experience ahead of you. This book is packed with well-tested techniques for alleviating anxiety, along with information that will expand your understanding of the various ways anxiety can show up in our lives. You won't find a more approachable book for treating your anxiety. The structure of the book embodies the spirit of CBT, as Arlin breaks down the program into manageable steps. As you follow Arlin's lead, you'll gain an understanding of where anxiety comes from and how CBT addresses it. And then, in typical CBT fashion, you'll roll up your sleeves and dive in. The program starts with setting clear goals. Then you'll learn how to identify and change unhelpful thoughts. You'll also practice new behaviors to diminish the power anxiety has over you. I'm delighted that Arlin chose to include principles of mindfulness in this program. Through this approach you'll learn how to find a more centered place of being by training your mind to focus on the present, with openness and curiosity.

Arlin will not only teach you techniques for managing your anxiety, she'll also explain how and why they work—and why some of the things we commonly do to cope with anxiety can actually backfire. By the end of the seven weeks, you'll have a set of tools you can use anytime you need them.

My client Susan and I used many of the approaches presented in this book. She invested a remarkable amount of time and energy in the work and took back the parts of her life she had sacrificed. In our final meeting she described a fundamental shift in her relationship with anxiety.

"It's not like I have to be scared of my fear," she told me. "Anxiety is always going to exist. The difference now is I know I can handle it."

For Susan, the realization that she was stronger than her fear was life changing. I hope and expect that after working your way through this book, you'll also have a different relationship with anxiety.

Letting go is not easy. Thankfully you've already taken the biggest step by committing to this 7-week program. When we decide we won't let anxiety hold us back—no matter what—we've already won. So trust your guide. Trust this program. And most of all, trust yourself. I wish you all the best for these 7 weeks and where they take you.

SETH J. GILLIHAN, PHD
Clinical Assistant Professor of Psychology, Department of Psychiatry,
Perelman School of Medicine, University of Pennsylvania
Author, *Retrain Your Brain: Cognitive Behavioral Therapy in 7 Weeks*

INTRODUCTION

Anxiety has a way of weaving itself into each part of a person's existence. Whether it takes the form of full-blown panic or chronic worry, anxiety can limit the potential of every aspect in your life. It might stop you from going to college, prevent you from finding a job, damage your relationships, or even make you a prisoner in your own home. In short, it can be truly incapacitating.

My first experience in helping someone overcome anxiety came during an undergraduate course in behavior therapy. I was assigned to help a student work through her fear of public speaking using a technique known as progressive muscle relaxation. Together, we constructed a list of her fears and worked on inducing a state of deep relaxation by having her alternatively tense and relax muscle groups in her body while she imagined herself in each of the situations she feared. Guiding her towards a place where she could cope with her anxiety in a short period of time was truly rewarding.

In late 2007, I was invited to create a website about anxiety for About.com (now Verywell.com). I'd completed a master's degree in clinical psychology five years earlier and was thrilled to have the chance to share knowledge and strategies with such a wide audience. Instead of helping one person at a time, I suddenly had the chance to positively impact tens of thousands of people every week.

In my role as a writer for the site, I have interviewed celebrities such as panic sufferer and reality show contestant Jamie Blyth (*The Bachelorette*) about his experience with anxiety. I also heard from readers who shared stories about their own issues with anxiety. I marveled at the ability of some to succeed despite the odds and felt empathy for the ones who did not know where to turn.

Prior to writing about anxiety, I worked for Dr. Zindel Segal at the Centre for Addiction and Mental Health in Toronto. Part of my job was doing intake with people wanting to participate in a study on the effectiveness of a treatment called cognitive behavioral therapy (CBT). Though the study focused on depression, many of those potential study participants were also coping with anxiety issues. Time and again, the individuals I talked to were eager to be placed in the therapy group. They would tell me they hoped they were one of the lucky ones who received CBT. I am here to tell you—you don't have to wait to be one of the lucky ones. Even if you don't yet have the means to attend therapy, the strategies that are learned during CBT can be accessible to everyone in the form of self-help.

Over the course of 10 years, while reviewing different anxiety treatments for my website, I read and scrutinized dozens of self-help books. What I found was that many books lacked a concrete timeline for the reader to follow in order to put the principles into practice. In other cases, there was a timeline to follow, but the plan was so unwieldy that it felt like the equivalent of taking a mini-course in psychological methods.

When you live with chronic worry or anxiety, it can be hard to feel motivated to get help. This is particularly true if you've been in treatment and not seen progress. You need practical, easy-to-follow solutions that give you a clear road map toward success.

That is where this book comes in. The focus of this anxiety workbook is on practice rather than theory. You won't find any long-winded explanations that leave you feeling overwhelmed or wondering what to do next. Rather than telling you what to do, this book will show you the strategies you can use to cope with anxiety.

My only request of you is that you make a commitment to see this plan through to the end. The chapters in Part Two of the book are structured to correspond to a period of 7 weeks, with each week building on what you have learned in the previous section. Over this period, you will identify your primary issues with anxiety and work through different strategies that you can use to reduce your symptoms and cope better.

This book is for everyone living with anxiety—whether you are currently in therapy, hesitant to start, or do not yet have the resources to receive outside help. While this book is not intended to replace a therapist, the strategies presented here are the same you would learn in treatment. Consider this book your accountability partner in a quest for good mental health and freedom from anxiety. You have completed the first important step of starting to read this book. I can't wait to get started.

Part One

GETTING STARTED

If you've made the choice to pick up this book, you are ready to embark on the journey toward feeling better. But before we start to unravel your anxiety, we first need to lay a foundation for the work to come.

In this section, we will learn where anxiety comes from and the different ways it can be expressed. We will also begin to explore the cognitive behavioral therapy (CBT) approach: learning where it came from and how it is used to treat anxiety. Throughout this section, a key theme will emerge—that of committing to taking action and following through. The process of overcoming anxiety takes time and you will face bumps in the road, but don't give up. If you follow the principles laid out in this book, you should see improvement within a short period of time.

Chapter One

Understanding Anxiety

In this chapter, we will explore and define anxiety, understand its different forms, and consider types of treatment for it. By the end, you will have an idea of the type of anxiety you are experiencing, how it manifests in your mind and body, and why it is important to take action to treat it.

Your Anxious Mind and Body

The fifth edition of the *Diagnostic and Statistical Manual of Mental Disorders* (*DSM-5*) defines anxiety as the "anticipation of future threat." People with anxiety experience tension, worry about potential threats, and avoid potentially dangerous situations. Let's consider an example as we work through what it means to have anxiety:

> *Samantha has not left home in six months. When she was employed, she would at least go out daily and maintain a routine. Now, she finds it nearly impossible. Routine activities, like buying groceries, reduce her to tears. She's experienced panic attacks before and is afraid to have them again—so she avoids places that might be triggers. It feels like her whole life revolves around her anxiety, fear, and avoidance.*

One rainy day, the doorbell rings while she is home alone and she feels herself start to panic. Her breathing becomes shallow and heart starts to race. Instead of going to open the door, she hides in her bedroom until the person leaves. It takes a very long time afterward for her to calm down.

While it seems like Samantha's anxiety is triggered by the doorbell in this situation, the process is a bit more complicated.

ANXIETY IN YOUR BRAIN

An anxiety attack starts with your sensory receptors: eyes, ears, nose. Imagine Samantha hearing the doorbell. Neurons in her brain stem begin to fire more intensely. Neurotransmitters such as norepinephrine send messages to parts of her brain shouting, "Alert, alert!" While a typical response to a ringing doorbell might be one of surprise or excitement and could involve some of the same initial brain processes, Samantha interprets her experience as anxiety, which starts a cycle that increases her level of arousal.

The messages sent to Samantha's brain are received by her amygdala and hippocampus. The amygdala lies deep in the brain, receives incoming signals, and alerts the rest of her brain to threats. It processes feelings, emotions, and fear quickly—without it, you would never feel anxiety.

In contrast, her hippocampus stores threatening experiences in her brain as memories and analyzes incoming threats in terms of past experience. When a threat is sensed, Samantha's hippocampus exchanges messages with other parts of her brain (such as her prefrontal cortex, which is responsible for planning) to decide whether to send a signal for her body to respond.

ANXIETY IN YOUR BODY

Once Samantha's brain decides to respond, her sympathetic nervous system is stimulated. Adrenaline and other hormones surge through her body. Her heart rate increases, blood pressure rises, and breathing becomes rapid. In the presence of an actual threat, her body is now prepared to fight or escape. Unfortunately for Samantha, there is no real physical threat and anxiety is the result.

Think about a situation in which you experienced anxiety—do you remember how you reacted? Were you confused or frightened by the feeling? Did you experience physical symptoms such as shaking or a racing heartbeat? Write down what you remember about the situation in the space below.

_____

_____

_____

_____

_____

Attention! If you're suffering from major depression or having immediate thoughts of suicide or self-harm, put this book down and visit your local hospital emergency room or call 911. If you are experiencing other major mental health issues, contact your mental health professional or primary doctor for assistance.

Where Does Anxiety Stem From?

Some people have anxious feelings their entire lives; others do not experience anxiety until after an event or trauma triggers it. Anxiety is thought to result from a combination of factors that differs for each person. Genetics are thought to play a role, as are aspects of your early development.

Have family members ever been diagnosed with anxiety? Twin studies are used to determine the role of genetics in anxiety disorders since identical twins share the same genes. A 2001 review of twin studies in the *American Journal of Psychiatry* found genetics contributed 30 to 40 percent toward the cause of anxiety disorders. This means that anxiety tends to run in families, and you are more likely to develop an anxiety disorder if someone in your family already has one.

Environmental factors are also thought to play a role in anxiety. Events during childhood such as abuse or an overly critical parent may trigger anxiety.

Life events that most people experience, such as moving, relationship problems, and loss of loved ones, may trigger anxiety in those who are already at risk due to their genetics. Having an anxious parent can also make you more likely to develop a problem with anxiety yourself, because you learn from watching your parent and eventually develop the same patterns of behavior.

Specific phobias, such as the fear of flying, often have a quick onset: a situation that previously did not cause you anxiety or discomfort suddenly becomes a source of fear. In this case, a sensitizing event such as bad turbulence on a flight may be the trigger. If you are already predisposed toward anxiety, your mind may have difficulty letting go of the memory of the event and cause you to be on guard for similar future threats.

Have you tried medication for your anxiety? If so, what was your experience like? Did you find that it improved your symptoms, and did the improvement last over the long term? If you have never taken anxiety medication, would you consider it? Write down any thoughts that you have about medication and your anxiety in the space below.

_____

_____

_____

_____

_____

_____

_____

_____

_____

_____

ON MEDICATION

Below are five classes of medication used for anxiety. These medications should only be taken under the supervision of a prescribing physician or psychiatrist.

Selective Serotonin Reuptake Inhibitors (SSRIs) such as fluoxetine (Prozac) block the reabsorption of the neurotransmitter serotonin, a brain chemical that contributes to feelings of well-being and happiness. These medications produce fewer side effects and are considered effective for all anxiety disorders.

Serotonin-Norepinephrine Reuptake Inhibitors (SNRIs) such as venlafaxine (Effexor) inhibit the neurotransmitters serotonin and norepinephrine, a brain chemical involved in feelings of alertness and energy, from being reabsorbed. These medications are considered as effective as SSRIs.

Benzodiazepines such as alprazolam (Xanax) are used in the short-term treatment of anxiety. They reduce physical symptoms by decreasing muscle tension.

Tricyclic Antidepressants such as imipramine (Tofranil) have been shown effective in the treatment of anxiety, but can have significant side effects, such as weight gain, drowsiness, and constipation.

Monoamine Oxidase Inhibitors (MAOIs) such as phenelzine (Nardil) block the effects of monoamine oxidase in the brain, which in turn helps boost neurotransmitters such as serotonin and norepinephrine. However, they have potentially serious side effects such as hypertensive crisis when combined with foods high in the compound tyramine (like aged cheeses and cured meats) and medications such as cough and cold medications and blood pressure medications.

Work with your doctor to determine which of these medications may be right for you. There may be a bit of trial and error involved, including adjusting dosage amounts or even the type of medication you're taking, before arriving at a working solution.

The Anxiety Checklist

This checklist will help determine the type of anxiety you are experiencing. Place a checkmark beside all statements that describe you.

CATEGORY A

☐ I have intense fear of a specific object/situation (e.g., snakes, heights).

☐ I almost always feel afraid when facing this object/situation.

☐ I try to avoid this object/situation; if I must face it, I feel intensely afraid.

☐ My fear seems out of proportion to the actual danger.

☐ I've had this fear for many months.

☐ This fear causes problems in my daily life.

CATEGORY B

☐ I have intense fear or anxiety about social/performance situations (e.g., meeting new people, giving a speech).

☐ In these situations, I'm afraid I will show anxiety (i.e., blushing or trembling) and people will think badly of me.

☐ I'm nearly always anxious or afraid in these situations.

☐ I try to avoid these situations or face them with intense fear.

☐ My fear seems too great for the actual threat in the situation.

☐ I've feared or avoided these situations for many months.

☐ This fear or avoidance creates problems in my daily life.

CATEGORY C

☐ I've experienced sudden episodes of intense and overwhelming fear that seemed to come out of the blue.

☐ During these episodes, I experienced four or more of the following symptoms: racing or pounding heart, sweating, shaking, breath-lessness, choking sensations, chest pain or discomfort, nausea or stomachache, dizziness or faintness, chills or feeling hot, numbness or tingling, feelings of unreality or detachment, feelings of loss of control or going crazy, or feeling afraid to die.

☐ I worry about having more episodes and try to avoid them (e.g., by avoiding exercise that might raise my heart rate or cause shortness of breath).

CATEGORY D

☐ I have intense fear of at least two of the following: public transpor-tation, open spaces, enclosed places, standing in line or in a crowd, or going out of my home alone.

☐ I fear or avoid these situations because it would be hard to escape or get help if I had a panic attack or emergency.

☐ These situations nearly always make me afraid.

☐ I avoid these situations or endure them with much anxiety.

☐ My fear seems out of proportion to the actual danger involved.

☐ I've feared these situations for many months.

☐ This fear causes problems in my daily life.

CATEGORY E

☐   I worry excessively about many things most days (e.g., job responsibilities, health, finances).

☐   I find it hard to control my worry.

☐   I've worried like this for several months.

☐   When I worry, I've experienced at least a few of the following: restlessness, being easily tired, trouble thinking, irritability, muscle tension, or trouble sleeping.

☐   These worries cause problems in my daily life.

RESULTS

Each category corresponds to a specific anxiety disorder. Check if your symptoms fall mostly in one or more categories.

☐   A: Specific phobia

☐   B: Social anxiety disorder

☐   C: Panic disorder

☐   D: Agoraphobia

☐   E: Generalized anxiety disorder

THE ANXIETY/FEAR CONNECTION

The *DSM-5* defines fear as an "emotional response to real or perceived imminent threat." When does fear run off the rails and become anxiety?

Fear can help alert us to danger but becomes anxiety when it is out of proportion to the situation. Feeling afraid about giving a public speech is natural. Most people do it anyway, learn that it is not dangerous, and feel less fear. In contrast, a person at risk for anxiety might feel such intense fear that, for example, avoiding public speaking seems necessary. Once avoided, the fear is lessened, and the person mistakenly thinks public speaking is the problem. Fear is no longer warning about danger; instead, anxiety is causing distress.

This book will help with all types of anxiety disorders, and we'll take a closer look at them individually in the following section. However, some may find it useful to join a support group for their specific type of anxiety. Consult the Resources section at the end of this book for more information.

Forms of Anxiety

Anxiety is not a one-size-fits-all disorder; it can manifest in many different ways. Below are five types of anxiety disorders. In each case, an anxiety disorder is only diagnosed when fear causes significant impairment in life and has been present for many months.

SPECIFIC PHOBIA

People with specific phobias fear objects or situations such as animals or heights. Most phobias are about things most people fear; however, the fear or anxiety is out of proportion to the actual danger in those with anxiety. A person with a fear of dogs might find it impossible to visit friends who own dogs. Someone with a fear of needles might avoid receiving important medical care. Specific phobias are diagnosed when the fear has a severe impact on a person's life over a period of several months.

SOCIAL ANXIETY DISORDER

People with social anxiety disorder (SAD) have an intense fear of being embarrassed or judged during social or performance situations like going to a party or giving a speech. They may fear blushing, shaking, or acting in ways that will make others think they are strange or anxious.

PANIC DISORDER

Panic disorder involves intense, unexpected episodes of panic with physical symptoms such as a racing heart, shortness of breath, chest pain, and dizziness. When these attacks first happen, the person may attribute them to a medical cause and visit the hospital looking for help. People with panic disorder may feel they are going crazy and worry about having more attacks.

AGORAPHOBIA

People with agoraphobia fear being in situations where escape or receiving help would be difficult if they were to have a panic attack, like in a crowded theater. In these situations, they may think: "What happens if I panic and can't leave?" Some people with agoraphobia feel better with a trusted friend or relative, while others stop leaving home completely. Most people with agoraphobia have lived with their fear for six months or longer.

GENERALIZED ANXIETY DISORDER

Generalized anxiety disorder (GAD) involves intense, chronic worry. People with GAD worry about health, finances, family members, having an accident—nearly everything. When one worry goes away, another takes its place. This type of worry persists over many months and is often accompanied by physical symptoms.

You Can Get Better

Trying cognitive behavioral therapy or other treatments for the first time can be daunting, especially if you feel you've tried everything and nothing has worked. Unraveling anxiety might feel like you're exposing yourself to more pain. However, the outcome is worth it. Below is a list of ways that overcoming anxiety will change your life.

• Your life goals will be easier to achieve. When you are no longer fearful and avoiding situations, you will feel free to pursue that promotion or take that once-in-a-lifetime trip. Goals that seemed out of reach will suddenly become realistic.

• You will think more positively about your future. Anxiety tends to cast a negative outlook on what is yet to come. When you are free of anxiety, you will feel more hopeful about what is around the next corner.

• It will be easier to cope with medical conditions. You won't worry unnecessarily about your physical health, but rather will do what is necessary to take care of yourself. Visits to the doctor will no longer fill you with anxiety and dread.

• You may feel relief from depression or low mood. When anxiety is relieved, depression and low mood often show improvement as well. Along with feeling less anxious, you may feel more optimistic, have more energy, sleep better, and generally have more interest in life.

• Anxiety will no longer define you as a person. If you have long-held beliefs about yourself that center around being anxious, those will be replaced with feelings of self-esteem and self-worth. You will get to know the person you can be without those anxious thoughts.

• You will take better care of yourself. Overcoming anxiety will shed light on areas of your life that have been neglected. You will give more importance to things like nutrition, exercise, and being present in the moment.

- Relationships and work that have suffered will improve. You might develop new social connections or feel less dependent on people you have leaned on in the past. Your increased ability to concentrate will make work seem like less of a chore, and you might even find yourself seeking advancement in the workplace.

- You will feel increased enjoyment in life and more confidence. Anxiety has a way of zapping your confidence and happiness. If you've felt like every day you were just "getting through," you will now start each day confidently and in search of joy.

Review and Reflect

In this chapter, we learned about causes of anxiety, effects on your mind and body, and different anxiety disorders. Going forward, please check in with yourself at the end of each chapter. Write down what you've learned and how you feel.

Which anxiety disorder describes you best? What motivates you to overcome your anxiety? Answers to these questions will help guide you through the remainder of this book.

_____

_____

_____

_____

_____

_____

_____

_____

_____

_____

_____

_____

_____

Chapter Two

The Cognitive Behavioral Approach

In this chapter, we'll learn about CBT, including how the approach was started, its main principles, and why it works. After reading this chapter, you should have a better understanding of how CBT might help with your anxiety.

First, let's examine what it means to have an anxiety attack through a scenario.

Dean is sitting in the window seat of the fifth row of a Boeing 737 jet on his way home from visiting family. The flight attendants are serving breakfast and their carts block the aisle. The passenger to his left has fallen asleep with his tray table open in front of him.

Dean's view out the window is of the landscape slowly fading away. The cabin is filled with the chatter of other passengers discussing their plans upon landing.

Unexpectedly, Dean begins to feel trapped. It's as though the walls of the airplane are closing in on him. His vision narrows, and he feels like he can't catch his breath. He turns to say something to the flight attendant in the aisle, but nothing comes out. He wants to stand up but his legs feel like cement blocks.

Terrified, Dean feels like he is suffocating. "If I don't get out of here right now, I am going to die," he thinks. By this point his heart is pounding in his ears, his arms are tingling, and he feels dizzy. "What if I'm having a heart attack?" he says to himself, breathing even more shallowly now.

Dean is terrified he is going to lose control, throw up, or pass out. The feeling continues for about 10 minutes and then slowly recedes, though he feels completely worn out the rest of the trip.

Afterward, Dean can't understand what happened. He makes an appointment with his doctor, sure there must be something wrong. He worries about the same thing happening again and starts avoiding places where he might feel trapped, like elevators and crowded events.

What Dean has experienced is a panic attack. During the attack, his thoughts about needing to escape or having a medical emergency only fueled his anxiety. In this way, we can view Dean's experience as a cycle.

DEAN'S PANIC LOOP

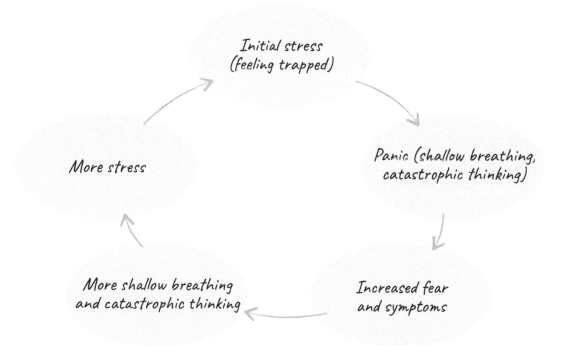

Initial stress
(feeling trapped)

Panic (shallow breathing, catastrophic thinking)

More stress

Increased fear
and symptoms

More shallow breathing
and catastrophic thinking

Had Dean known about the principles of CBT, he would have recognized the connection between his thoughts and anxious feelings and learned to break the loop after the initial stress. To understand how CBT could have helped Dean, let's look at how it developed and its main principles.

CBT: A Brief History

The roots of CBT date all the way back to Ancient Greece. For example, the Greek philosopher Epictetus, who overcame significant obstacles on his own path to success, believed that logic could be used to identify and discard false beliefs that lead to destructive emotions. However, it wasn't until the 1980s that cognitive behavioral therapy first became popular.

EARLY FOUNDATIONS

They say necessity is the mother of invention, and the early beginnings of CBT were no different. By the end of the 1940s, a surge of World War II veterans were suffering from anxiety and depression, and therapists were seeking short-term treatments. Freudian psychoanalytic therapy, the most common treatment at that time, was no longer serving the needs of clients or therapists. Psychological treatment was on the brink of change.

Let's back up a bit. You've probably heard of Russian physiologist Ivan Pavlov. In the 1890s, he identified the concept of the conditioned reflex. In his lab, he showed that dogs who were fed at the sound of a bell unconsciously learned to salivate when the bell rang. Pavlov's work was pivotal in that it showed how fear might be conditioned. Then, in 1920, American psychologist John B. Watson extended on Pavlov's research. In the "Little Albert" experiment, he showed that a child could learn to fear furry animals when they were paired with a loud noise. Later, American psychologist B. F. Skinner, with his theory of operant conditioning, showed how behavior could be shaped through reward and punishment.

By the 1950s and 1960s, a new treatment based on these principles, known as behavior therapy, was established simultaneously in several parts of the world. Early behavioral techniques focused on increasing exposure to feared objects or situations, such as systematic desensitization developed by South African psychiatrist Joseph Wolpe. To this day, behavioral techniques remain an important component of CBT.

SECOND WAVE

By the late 1960s, the field of psychology was ready for more change. The importance of thoughts (cognitions) in emotions and behavior had been recognized and the cognitive revolution began to take shape. With the cognitive revolution, therapists now considered patients' thoughts instead of just their behavior. Instead of imagining people as Pavlov's dogs, reacting directly to an external event, it was acknowledged that thoughts were the link between external events and feelings and behaviors.

In this way, CBT aimed at changing not just behavior, but also beliefs, attitudes, thinking styles, and expectations. During the 1980s and 1990s, cognitive and behavioral techniques merged to form this new type of therapy. Influential figures during this time included American psychologist Albert Ellis, the founder of rational emotive behavior therapy (REBT), and the father of cognitive therapy, American psychiatrist Aaron T. Beck.

THIRD WAVE

With the new millennium, CBT morphed again. During what is known as the third wave, therapists considered the process of thinking itself, rather than simply the content of thoughts, when devising treatment. If I asked you right now not to think about chocolate cake, what's the first thing that comes to mind? Eating a decadent slice, of course. According to this new wave of CBT, trying to control thoughts and emotions was counterproductive. During this time, new therapies such as acceptance and commitment therapy (ACT) and dialectical behavior therapy (DBT) emerged, which incorporated the role of acceptance and mindfulness into traditional CBT.

Regardless of the specific techniques used, CBT has become the staple form of treatment for a multitude of mental disorders. In the next section, we will explore the CBT approach and why it works.

How and Why

The main principles of CBT can be divided into two overall themes: active collaboration and structured problem solving. You'll notice as we discuss various characteristics of CBT that the emphasis is on time-based treatment. Given the structured nature of this therapy, most clients will conclude their treatment within several weeks to a few months. Let's have a closer look at these two aspects of CBT.

ACTIVE COLLABORATION

Collaborative. Imagine attending treatment with a therapist who lectures and devalues you. Even if the treatment is helpful, you would leave feeling no more in control of your own ability to cope. In contrast, during CBT the therapist and client collaborate in a quest for change. This process depends on a good *therapeutic alliance*; CBT therapists are empathic, caring, good listeners, proud of your successes, and ask for your feedback. They identify how thoughts and behaviors contribute to anxiety through a process called *guided discovery*. This involves exploring evidence, checking whether thoughts are valid, uncovering automatic thoughts, and developing more adaptive responses—together.

Education-based. CBT clients don't just practice new skills. They also learn about their anxiety disorders and the model underlying CBT. Education is an important aspect of this type of therapy.

Active and skills-oriented. During CBT, the therapist and client decide together what to work on, how often to meet, and what to do for homework. Over time, the client takes on a more active role and learns skills to prevent relapse once finished with treatment.

Emphasizes practice. You can't turn off your brain for an hour each week and let someone else fix you in CBT. You've got to do work to benefit from this type of therapy.

STRUCTURED PROBLEM-SOLVING

Focus on the present. Rather than focusing on the causes of your distress, CBT works to reduce it in the present. The past only becomes important to discuss if it is keeping you stuck with your problems.

Time-limited. Most clients with mild to moderate issues can be helped in 6 to 20 sessions. Booster sessions at the end of treatment are also sometimes used to maintain what you've learned, but CBT is time-based treatment.

Structured. Each CBT session follows a structured format: check-in, review of the previous week, current week's agenda, homework review, current week's problems, setting new homework, summarizing, and getting feedback. In this way, clients know what to expect and can use the same principles on their own after treatment.

Evidence-based. CBT uses a variety of techniques that have been validated and shown to work. The therapist chooses CBT methods that are known to work best for the issues faced by a specific client.

WHY IT WORKS

In many ways, clients treated with CBT are set up for success from the start. Let's think back to Dean.

Dean's doctor ran all the necessary medical tests but found nothing wrong. Dean returned to his daily life but soon had another attack while at work. Suspecting that Dean was having panic attacks, his doctor suggested meeting with a cognitive behavioral therapist to learn about the connection between his thoughts, feelings, and behaviors. Dean was wary of being in psychological treatment but decided to give it a try.

OTHER TYPES OF TREATMENT

Beyond traditional CBT, several other types of therapy may be used to treat anxiety.

Acceptance and Commitment Therapy (ACT) was developed in 1986 by psychology professor Steven Hayes and has roots in Buddhist philosophy. The goal of ACT is to help the client learn to accept negative thoughts rather than eliminate them. The principles of ACT include cognitive defusion (separating yourself from anxious thoughts), acceptance, mindfulness, self-observation, identification of values, and taking committed action toward goals.

Dialectical Behavior Therapy (DBT) integrates CBT techniques with concepts based on Eastern meditation with a goal of achieving acceptance and change. Designed in the late 1980s by psychologist Marsha Linehan, DBT focuses on how the person interacts with others. During DBT, clients learn about mindfulness, interpersonal skills, tolerating distress, and regulating emotions. DBT is typically used for more severe issues and usually involves group therapy.

Interpersonal Therapy (IPT) is a short-term treatment developed by Gerald Klerman and Myrna Weissman in the 1980s. IPT focuses on the social context of disorders and improving interpersonal functioning. In this way, IPT may be particularly suited to social anxiety disorder.

Eye Movement Desensitization and Reprocessing (EMDR) is sometimes used to treat panic attacks and phobias through a process similar to dreaming or rapid eye movement (REM) sleep. Through EMDR, clients learn to view disturbing events in a less distressing way.

Psychoanalysis is based on psychodynamic theory originated by Sigmund Freud. The goal of this long-term therapy is to uncover and work through underlying conflicts believed to cause disorders.

Given Dean's trepidation about therapy, it is fortunate his doctor suggested CBT. Dean would be an active participant in this treatment and trained to use strategies on his own. In this way, Dean would feel valued and understood in this sort of therapist-client relationship. With practice, Dean would begin to adopt new thoughts and behaviors in his daily life. The more these new ways of acting and thinking were practiced, the easier it would become for him to adopt them as his new way of interacting with the world.

Dean would also be happy to learn that no time would be wasted. Therapy would be short-term, and he would feel motivated to come back each week and complete treatment. Inevitably, after finishing treatment, Dean would face new issues. However, what he learned in CBT would help him develop better ways to react.

Motivation for Change

Some people struggle with motivation for change related to their anxiety. Maybe the obstacles seem too large. Normally, people go through five stages when planning a change:

Precontemplation: In the precontemplation stage, you are thinking that it is possible to reduce your anxiety but have not yet committed to making a change.

Contemplation: At the contemplation stage, you are planning to work on reducing your anxiety sometime in the future but have not yet taken any action toward doing so.

Preparation: In the preparation stage, you are actively planning how you will reduce your anxiety in the near future.

Action: During the action stage, you are actively working on making a change related to your anxiety.

Maintenance: In the maintenance stage, you are working on not falling back into old patterns of anxious thoughts and behaviors.

If you're reading this, you've likely already moved through the first two stages and are actively planning to tackle your anxiety. If you are still finding it hard to commit to change, ask yourself the following questions and write your answers in the space provided:

What are the pros/cons of treating your anxiety?

_____

_____

_____

_____

_____

_____

What will your life look like 20 years from now if you still have anxiety? How will it look if you don't?

_____

_____

_____

_____

_____

_____

Committing to Wellness

Though I've tried to make this workbook as simple as I can, it is still up to you to do the work. It's likely that over the next seven weeks, life will throw you some curveballs—please don't let this deter you. Make time for this, just like you try to make time for exercise, eating well, and getting enough rest. Your mental health deserves just as much of your attention.

Schedule time each week to read through one chapter and do the exercises. Mark an X on your calendar once when you've completed each week. Circle your end date in red so that you have a deadline. Remember, it's only seven weeks. The time is going to pass anyway; you might as well be making progress.

COMPLEMENTARY INTERVENTIONS

Be sure to check with your primary doctor or mental health professional before engaging in any of these complementary interventions for anxiety.

Relaxation techniques such as mindfulness meditation, progressive muscle relaxation, controlled breathing, and visualization have been shown effective for treating anxiety.

Biofeedback is an evidence-based treatment that involves teaching the client awareness of the anxiety response, relaxation skills, and how to control the brain's activity.

Hypnotherapy was recognized by the American Medical Association (AMA) in 1958 as a valid medical procedure. Its goal is to separate the anxiety response from external triggers.

Supplements such as valerian root, passionflower, chamomile, and others are sometimes used in treating anxiety. However, these are not regulated by the US Food and Drug Administration.

Aromatherapy involves the use of essential oils to calm anxiety.

Acupuncture uses a thin, sharp needle inserted into upper layers of the skin at points of the body corresponding to different organs to activate natural painkillers in the brain.

Review and Reflect

In this chapter, we learned about cognitive behavioral therapy, how and why it works, and complementary treatments for anxiety. We also discussed your motivation to change and why it is important that you commit to taking action and following this plan through to completion. At this point, take a moment to check in with yourself. What have you learned and how do you feel about what we've covered in this chapter? Write a few notes to keep yourself on track and moving forward.

_____

_____

_____

_____

_____

_____

_____

_____

_____

_____

_____

_____

_____

Part Two

TAKING ACTION

Now that we've covered the basics, it's time to begin applying the CBT approach. This part of the book is organized into seven chapters, each one corresponding to one week of the program you will follow. These chapters will require you to interact with what you read by answering questions and applying what you learn. It does not matter whether you work through each chapter in one sitting or spread out the lessons over a few days. However, be sure to complete the exercises in order, as you will be building on what you learn in earlier sections.

At the end of each chapter, I have also listed a few activities for you to complete before moving on to the following week. The cornerstone of CBT is repetition. The more you practice identifying and evaluating your thoughts, the better you will become at doing it. Our goal by the end of this book is for you to have tools to continue applying CBT principles on your own when anxiety arises. Ready? Then let's get started.

Week One

What Ails You?

In the previous chapter, we learned about the cognitive behavioral approach to treating anxiety, including the history of CBT and why it works. We also discussed motivation to change and committing to wellness.

Before we get started on the nuts and bolts of CBT, it is important to consider the goals you hope to achieve by working on your anxiety. To set goals, we must first examine your core issues with anxiety and specific symptoms. Each person possesses a unique set of issues—even two people with the same anxiety diagnosis.

Anne is sitting slumped at her desk, her head in her hands. A concerned coworker gently taps her on the shoulder. "Are you okay?" This isn't the first time others at work have noticed her looking strained. Around the office, she is known as a worrier.

While she excels at her job, Anne's constant worry interferes with how she goes about each day. "Will I be late this morning?" "Am I going to be fired?" "What if I become ill or my husband loses his job?" "How will we pay the bills?" "What if my children are injured?" These types of thoughts constantly cycle through her head, making it hard to concentrate and get things done.

Between her migraines, body aches, and inability to sleep, Anne feels worn out. Her husband is also losing patience with her. She's been working late so often that they rarely talk anymore.

Picking up on her distress, Anne's supervisor puts her in contact with their Employee Assistance Program (EAP). Through the EAP, she meets with a therapist, and together they discuss the problems she has been having. Anne learns that her symptoms fit the profile of generalized anxiety disorder.

She shares with her therapist that she feels her worry will never go away. Her therapist understands her concerns and assures her he's had great success using short-term cognitive behavioral therapy with clients in the past who've had similar worries. They make a plan to meet for seven weekly sessions and then evaluate her progress.

Getting to Know Your Anxiety

What symptoms of your anxiety bother you most? What areas of your life have been most affected by your anxiety? Identifying your unique symptoms and the areas in which you need help is a key step in defining your goals.

Take a moment to write down your feelings. Are there a few areas of your life that you feel need the most attention? What types of anxiety symptoms make life hardest for you? Think of a recent situation in which you experienced anxiety and write down aspects of the situation that stand out in your mind.

_____

_____

_____

_____

_____

_____

PHYSICAL SYMPTOMS

Anne tends to carry her anxious feelings in her body. She has a lot of muscle tension and headaches, and becomes tired easily. She also has difficulty sleeping—some nights she lies awake for hours worrying and unable to fall asleep.

Think back to your most recent experience with anxiety. What feelings did you have? We discussed some of these symptoms when outlining the different types of anxiety disorders. Check the symptoms that are most severe for you or cause the most distress in your daily life.

- Blurry vision
- Blushing
- Chest pain
- Chills or hot flashes
- Crying
- Choking feeling
- Dizziness or lightheadedness
- Dry mouth
- Excessive sweating
- Fatigue
- Feelings of unreality or being detached

- Headaches
- Muscle tension
- Nausea or diarrhea
- Numbness or tingling
- Racing or pounding heart
- Shaky voice
- Shortness of breath or smothering feeling
- Trembling or shaking
- Trouble sleeping
- Other: _____

COGNITIVE SYMPTOMS

For as long as she can remember, Anne has been a worrier. Though she tries to relax, she always feels on edge and restless. She also notices that her anxiety influences her thoughts—sometimes when she is talking with coworkers her mind goes completely blank.

Cognitive symptoms refer to your mental experiences of anxiety. These symptoms vary depending on your specific type of anxiety. If you have panic disorder, you fear that you will go crazy. If you have social anxiety disorder, you worry that other people are judging you in a negative way.

Reflect on your most recent anxious experience. What thoughts passed through your mind? How did anxiety affect your concentration or mood? Check the symptoms below that apply to you, and write in any that are not included.

- I worried others were judging me.

- I was afraid of being embarrassed or humiliated.

- I dreaded an upcoming social or performance event.

- I felt like things would always end badly.

- I felt keyed up and restless.

- I was afraid of losing control or going crazy.

- I was afraid of dying.

- I was afraid I could not escape if I panicked.

- I had a feeling of impending doom.

- I felt the need to escape.

- I had trouble concentrating.

- My mind went blank.

- I was irritable.

- I lacked confidence.

- I felt unable to cope.

- I felt hopeless.

- I felt like I could not control my worry.

- Other: _____

BEHAVIORAL SYMPTOMS

In the office, Anne is known as a perfectionist. She arrives much earlier than necessary due to her fear of being late. She relentlessly reviews her work to catch mistakes and often works much longer hours than everyone else in her department. Her constant need for reassurance is also creating problems in her marriage. It's gotten to the point that her husband lets her calls go to voicemail, because he can no longer cope with her constant check-ins.

Anxiety does not only express itself in how you feel and what you think—it is also reflected in your behavior. If you have panic disorder, you might avoid taking elevators due to fear of having a panic attack and not being able to escape. If you have a phobia of snakes, you could decide vacations to tropical destinations are out of the question. Social anxiety might cause you to avoid parties or other social engagements. Below are some ways anxiety can show itself in your behaviors. Think back to the situation you identified at the start of this section, check the behaviors below that are true for you, and write in any that are not listed.

- I avoided things or situations that I feared.

- I overcompensated by working extra hard.

- I left or escaped from a situation.

- I did things to distract myself or not feel anxious (e.g., not looking someone in the eye).

- I sought reassurance from other people.

- Other: _____

"Everything can be taken from a man but one thing: the last of the human freedoms—to choose one's attitude in any given set of circumstances."
—*Victor E. Frankl, Austrian psychiatrist*

Behavioral Approach Test

Therapists sometimes use a technique called the behavioral approach test (BAT) to make it easier to identify physical, cognitive, and behavioral symptoms of anxiety. Using this technique, you would enter a feared situation and then immediately afterward make notes about your anxious symptoms and behaviors.

Anne's therapist asked her to leave for work at 8:00 a.m. instead of her usual 7:30 a.m., so that they could observe her anxious reaction. It was still plenty of time to get there by 9:00 a.m., which was her actual start time. Once she arrived at work, Anne jotted down what she had felt that morning leaving at the later time. She noted that her body felt tense and she was worried about not getting to work on time. She had called her husband asking for reassurance, and by the time she arrived at work, a headache had started. She felt so on edge that she had to sit in the women's restroom for a few minutes before she went to her desk. On a scale of 0 to 10, she rated her anxiety a 10 by the time she started working.

In some cases, facing a feared situation could be too anxiety provoking. Instead, your therapist would use a role-playing technique to assess your anxiety. In Anne's case, she and her therapist would act out her morning routine with her leaving for work at the later time. This would also give her therapist the chance to directly observe her anxious reaction while in the imagined scenario.

If you are having trouble identifying your anxiety symptoms, try engaging in a behavioral approach test on your own. Enter a situation that you fear, and then immediately afterward record your anxious feelings, thoughts, and behaviors. If that seems too daunting, conduct a role-play in which you imagine yourself entering the situation. Write down any observations you have about this exercise in the space below.

SAFETY BEHAVIORS

You may find yourself using safety behaviors to reduce fear and anxiety when you feel threatened. While these actions reduce your anxiety in the short term, they prolong it over the long term. For example, if you have social anxiety disorder, you might reduce your anxiety by never voicing your opinion. In doing so, you learn that the only way to get through social situations is to keep quiet. You never get the chance to test out that belief—and discover whether it could be wrong. Safety behaviors can be obvious or subtle; some examples are listed below.

- Avoiding situations such as not leaving the house
- Needing a trusted companion along with you for support in case of a panic attack
- Escaping from situations that make you feel anxious, such as leaving a party early
- Subtle behaviors such as looking at a cell phone or over-rehearsing a presentation
- Seeking constant reassurance from others
- Distracting yourself from a threatening situation, such as by reading a book before a presentation
- Doing things in situations to not fully experience your anxiety, such as not looking when getting a shot or holding a railing tightly in a high place
- Carefully monitoring your bodily symptoms in an effort to control them

Anxiety Triggers

When Anne was uncertain about situations, she felt anxious and worried. Not knowing what traffic would be like on the freeway, feeling unsure if her supervisor was happy with her work, and the possibility of family members becoming ill kept her up at night. It seemed she could worry about almost any-thing. She worried about current situations, like whether they would be able to pay the bills, and hypothetical problems, like one of them being diagnosed with an incurable illness.

Understanding your anxiety triggers—those situations that lead to your experience of anxiety—is a key part of planning treatment. While some of your anxiety may seem to be free-floating and not linked to any specific trigger, it's likely that some of your symptoms show up in a predictable manner.

In the case of specific phobias, anxiety triggers are usually easy to identify. If you fear heights, you will feel anxious on a high floor of a building. If you are afraid of needles, you will feel rising panic while waiting for a flu shot.

Social anxiety disorder triggers include a variety of social and perfor-mance situations. Talking to strangers, meeting new people, asking someone on a date, expressing your opinion, or going on a job interview are common anxiety-provoking situations. Common performance triggers include eating or drinking in front of others, writing in front of others, public speaking, and using a public restroom.

In the case of panic disorder, the triggers of anxiety include bodily sen-sations and your interpretation of them. If you have panic disorder, you are probably finely tuned in to the feelings in your body and interpret them in a catastrophic way. Chest pain is interpreted as a heart attack. Trouble catching your breath turns into hyperventilation. Fear that your physical symptoms are a sign of an underlying health condition is a common trigger in panic disorder.

If you have agoraphobia, your anxiety is likely triggered by situations in which you perceive that escape would be difficult if you had a panic attack, including riding on public transportation, being in open or closed spaces, standing in crowds or lines, and being out of your house alone.

What situations or things do you fear or avoid? What aspects of these objects or situations make your anxiety worse? Do you remember the first time you felt very worried or had an anxiety attack? Think about what was happening at the time and any unique aspects of the situation. Write what you remember in the space below.

_____

_____

_____

_____

_____

_____

_____

_____

_____

_____

_____

_____

Research tells us that about 9 percent of people live with a specific phobia and that phobias are twice as common in women as in men. Most people first develop their fear in childhood or adolescence, and it lasts through adulthood. In the United States, fear of animals is the most common specific phobia, with dogs, snakes, and bugs topping the list of feared creatures. Less commonly, some people may even fear things that have no inherent aspect of danger—such as clowns or balloons.

Areas of Concern

We've talked a lot about specific anxiety symptoms. I'd also like to know about various areas of your life and how they relate to your anxiety. Life quality is often reduced because of anxiety. Sometimes, life experiences may also trigger or aggravate anxiety, such as working at a stressful job or going through a divorce. Your current life situation is the context in which your anxiety has continued, so it's important for us to consider.

Let's take a moment now to take stock of each aspect of your life. I'd like you to reflect on how you are doing, where you feel you need improvement, and ways in which anxiety has taken a toll.

SOCIAL INTERACTIONS

Anne knows that her anxiety is creating problems with her marriage and in her friendships. Her constant need for reassurance about even the smallest things has driven people away from her—including those closest to her. "I just wish I could kick back and relax like everyone else," she thinks. "Then they would see I still have some fun left in me."

Anxiety can cause problems in your relationships—and relationship struggles may also worsen your anxiety. Social anxiety may cause you to feel isolated. It makes it hard to forge new friendships. Panic attacks may leave you feeling ashamed. Often the stigma of having anxiety can create as much of a burden as the anxiety symptoms themselves. On top of this, relationship problems can contribute to anxiety. Stressful situations such as going through a divorce can create new worries that add to your burden and make it hard to cope.

Think about your own life. How has anxiety had an impact on your relationships? Depending on who is present in your life, you might think about your family, friends, romantic partner, or children. Do you have a confidant?

Are you going through any transitions in your relationships? Do you struggle to make new friends? Record your thoughts in the space below.

_____

_____

_____

_____

_____

_____

_____

_____

_____

_____

_____

_____

_____

EDUCATION AND WORK

Anne knew that her anxiety was interfering with her job. In addition to compulsively checking her work, she had also been passed over for a promotion because of the perception that she was "too anxious" and "made others nervous."

In what ways has anxiety had an impact on your education or career? Do you worry constantly about work responsibilities? Have you dropped out of school or quit a job because of a fear of leaving the house? Have you avoided taking classes or working at a job where public speaking is necessary? Has stress at work contributed to your anxiety?

Think about how anxiety has impacted your education or career. How do you feel about your current school or work situation? Record your thoughts in the space below.

_____

_____

_____

_____

_____

_____

_____

_____

HEALTH AND WELL-BEING

Anne was suffering physically and mentally. She had regular headaches that seemed to worsen when she was anxious. As a child she enjoyed playing sports, but as an adult she rarely took part in any physical exercise. Some worry always came along that interfered with her taking part in life. She often felt depressed and like things would never change. It was as though she was just trying to get through each day.

Anxiety can have a negative impact on your health and well-being. It may impair your ability to maintain your physical health, such as following a proper diet or getting regular exercise. Health problems can also make anxiety issues worse—such as asthma attacks triggering panic symptoms. Migraines and irritable bowel syndrome also tend to go along with anxiety and may cause you distress. You may even have overlapping mental health issues, such as depression or substance abuse, which can make overcoming anxiety that much more difficult.

Let's think for a moment about your overall health and well-being. Have you been diagnosed with any medical conditions or other mental health conditions that might contribute to your anxiety? How is your sleep? Do you eat healthy foods? Exercise regularly? Anxiety can impact all of these areas of your life, and they can also impact your anxiety, so it's important to consider how you are doing. Write your thoughts below.

_____

_____

_____

_____

_____

_____

DAILY RESPONSIBILITIES

Anne found daily tasks difficult. From the moment she got up in the morning, she was focused on what could go wrong. It was hard for her to concentrate on household responsibilities and it took her much too long to do routine things, such as choosing her clothes for the day.

This category includes things you probably do daily, such as driving a car, making meals, personal care, paying bills, cleaning the house, choosing clothes to wear, and so on. Anxiety can have an impact on your ability to do the most basic tasks.

How is your ability to meet the demands of each day? Does anxiety interfere with you getting things done? Are your days so busy and stressful that they make your anxiety worse? Record your thoughts in the space below.

_____

_____

_____

_____

_____

_____

OTHER FACTORS

Are there any other areas of your life that we have not touched on, such as your financial situation, housing issues, feelings of safety and security, or time for leisure activities? Think about how these could relate to your anxiety and record your thoughts below.

For example, have you faced any recent financial struggles? Are you comfortable with where you live? Do you have any reason to feel unsafe in your environment? Do you have time for leisure and recreation, and are you able to enjoy it? Record your thoughts about other factors that could be contributing to your anxiety below.

_____

_____

_____

_____

_____

Goal Setting

Are you ready to get started setting your goals? Personally, I am excited we are at this point in the process. This is where we start to take actions to help you tackle your anxiety. Goals are critical to the process as they allow you to see whether you have made progress. They can involve short-term gains or long-term changes and may be general in nature or laser-focused on a specific concern.

Short-term goals are those that you could achieve within the next week, medium-range goals might take a few weeks, and long-range goals are those you anticipate reaching within the next year or two.

Goals may also be general or specific. Specific goals are useful when planning activities during treatment, while general goals consider the broad picture of what you hope to achieve over the course of therapy.

For example, Anne chose the following general goals with a medium-range time frame (by the end of treatment):

1. Feel less anxious and worried in her daily life.

2. Work more reasonable hours.

3. Improve her relationship with her husband.

4. Improve her self-confidence.

5. Feel better in terms of her physical health.

Based on these general goals, she generated specific short-term goals in treatment, such as working no more than 40 hours per week and exercising for 30 minutes three times a week.

GOALS LIST

Now it's your turn. Look back over what we've discussed in this chapter, including your physical, cognitive, and behavioral symptoms, and their impacts on various areas of your life. Considering the key themes that emerge, come up with four to six general goals that you hope to achieve by the end of this program. Write these down in the space below. Don't worry about coming up with specific goals at this time—we will consider those in a later chapter.

_____

_____

_____

_____

_____

_____

_____

_____

_____

_____

_____

"Many people fail in life, not for lack of ability or brains or even courage, but simply because they have never organized their energies around a goal."
—American philosopher Elbert Hubbard

S.M.A.R.T. GOALS

Have you heard of S.M.A.R.T. goals? The S.M.A.R.T. goals acronym refers to goals that are specific, measurable, action-oriented, realistic, and time-based.

Specific. These types of goals are well-defined and easy to understand. When your goal is specific, it is easier to determine what you need to do to achieve it. For example, the general goal "feel less anxious" could be translated into the specific goal "deliver a speech to my class without feeling significant anxiety."

Measurable. If a goal is not measurable, it's hard to know when it has been achieved. An example of a measurable goal would be keeping an anxiety diary for a week to develop an understanding of your feelings and thoughts.

Action-oriented. Goals should state actions that are required to make progress. For example, your goal could be to feel less anxious around dogs. However, this general goal doesn't state any actions that need to be taken. An action-oriented goal would be: "visit a neighbor's house who has a dog in the next week."

Realistic. It isn't helpful to have a goal that you can never hope to achieve. For example, it isn't realistic that you will never have another anxious thought. A more realistic goal would be to accept that you will sometimes have anxious thoughts, but that you have a plan to manage them.

Time-based. Well-formed goals are time-based. This means that you have set a time frame for them to be achieved to keep you focused. Examples could include leaving the house or saying hello to your neighbor once in the coming week.

Worry Diary

A Worry Diary is a helpful tool to keep track of how often you encounter situations that cause anxiety, what you feel in those situations, how you react, and the level of your distress. Below you will find a sample Worry Diary completed by someone with social anxiety disorder.

At the end of this chapter, you will find a Worry Diary form for you to complete over the next week. Each time you experience significant anxiety, record the date and time, situation, a rating of your fear or anxiety from 0 to 10, and any physical sensations you experienced, thoughts you had, and actions you took. Remember, sometimes actions can involve avoidance, such as leaving a situation. Try to complete the form shortly after experiencing the event, so that you can easily remember what happened. Plan to complete this form each time you encounter a feared situation over the next week.

WORRY DIARY

DATE/TIME	SITUATION	ANXIETY RATING (0–10)	FEELINGS, THOUGHTS, ACTIONS
Sat. April 1, 2017, at 10:00 a.m.	At the park with my children	8	Felt like my heart was pounding, thought other parents must see I am nervous, avoided talking to them
Sat. April 1, 2017, at 8:00 p.m.	At a friend's house, meeting someone for the first time	7	Hands shaking, blushing, feel like I need to escape, avoided eye contact
Mon. April 3, 2017, at 10:00 a.m.	Asked a question in a work meeting	10	Shortness of breath, pounding heart, rushed through my answer, spoke too softly, thought "What if I make a fool of myself?"

Addressing Doubt

Are you feeling doubtful whether CBT will work or wondering if it is right for you? If so, let's take a moment to address your concerns. CBT has been proven effective in the treatment of anxiety, but it takes commitment on your part. If you've been in therapy for anxiety before or tried a self-help program without success, you may wonder why this time will be any different. Let's take a moment and review your history of anxiety treatment.

In the space below, record any other types of therapy you have received and any self-help books that you used. Describe how long each lasted and whether you experienced any improvement. If they did not help, can you think of any reasons why? If you met with a therapist, did you feel valued in that relationship? If you used a self-help book, did you put the principles into practice?

_____

_____

_____

_____

_____

_____

_____

_____

_____

_____

_____

Now let's consider your impression of the CBT approach. In general, how do you feel about CBT so far? Are you willing to invest time each week to putting these principles to work? Do you think that this approach makes sense and that it could work for you? Make some notes here about your thoughts on CBT and what you expect to achieve by completing the exercises in this book.

_____

_____

_____

_____

_____

_____

_____

YOUR STRENGTHS

It's easy to become focused on your faults when you are anxious. When you are wrapped up in what you've done wrong, what you will do wrong, and what could possibly go wrong, your strengths have trouble rising to the surface. But every person has different strengths that can be used to help overcome even the worst situations. In the case of Anne, her work was highly regarded; once her anxiety was under control, a promotion was likely to be offered.

If you have lived with anxiety for a long time, it could be hard to think of good things about yourself. To help you with this task, think of the following. What are you good at? Perhaps you have an eye for detail or are a natural organizer. Have you overcome any significant challenges in your life, such as learning to cope with a medical condition? How have you helped others or made them happy, perhaps by being a good listener or offering advice? Do you have any unique qualities, such as a quirky sense of humor?

Finally, what do you value the most? For example, I value time spent with my family, traveling, and learning new things. Write your thoughts about all of these questions in the space below.

_____

_____

_____

_____

_____

_____

_____

_____

Through this process, it will be helpful to draw on your strengths. For example, Anne's attention to detail and analytical mind made it easy for her to complete the Worry Diary form and keep up with her homework. Whatever strengths you have, see if you can draw on them as you work through your anxiety.

Review and Reflect

In this chapter, we've discussed your issues with anxiety and devised a handful of general goals. In the coming chapters, we will be working on specific goals related to your anxious symptoms.

For now, I would like you to review the goals you have listed and make a commitment to come back for week 2. Don't forget to complete the Worry Diary for anxiety-provoking situations over the coming week.

Now is also a good time to check in with yourself. Write down your thoughts about what you've read this week.

_____

_____

_____

_____

_____

_____

_____

_____

_____

_____

_____

_____

_____

_____

ACTIVITY PLAN

1. Review your goal list.

2. Schedule a time to return for week 2.

3. Complete the Worry Diary for at least three situations.

DATE/TIME	SITUATION	ANXIETY RATING (0–10)	FEELINGS, THOUGHTS, ACTIONS

Identify Your Thought Patterns

In the last section, we examined your anxiety symptoms and how different areas of your life relate to your anxiety. Then we set some general goals that you are seeking to achieve by the end of this program. I also asked you to keep a Worry Diary, in which you recorded situations that made you anxious—you wrote down what you felt, thought, and did during each of those events.

How did things go with your Worry Diary? Did you have trouble identifying how you were feeling or what you were thinking? Don't spend too much time on this—we're going to dig deeper in the second part of this section to identify the thoughts that come between situations and your anxious reactions. First, I'd like to start by examining the different ways that thoughts can be unhelpful when you have anxiety.

Unhelpful Thoughts

Jack couldn't remember ever having friends growing up. At least not his own. Jack's twin brother John was the sociable one in the family, so Jack tended to follow in his shadow. He'd done the same in following him to college, but now it all felt like a big mistake.

It was the middle of the second semester of college when Jack finally admitted he needed help. His grades were slipping from missing class, and he'd hardly left his dorm room. One day, as he walked back to his room from biology class, he took a detour into the student center and made an appointment at the counseling office.

Though he was intelligent, Jack had missed out on opportunities because of his anxiety. He was too fearful to apply for job postings he saw on campus. When it came to giving presentations in his class, he pretended to be ill so that he did not have to participate. The thought of speaking in front of the class made him feel nauseous and dizzy. "There is no way I could get through that," Jack thought.

Jack's anxiety was not just related to speaking in front of the class. He was also afraid of having to talk to other students. He would wait until he was sure nobody was in the hall before he left his room, so that he didn't have to make conversation.

Everyone called him "quiet," but Jack knew they thought even worse, that he was unlikable and weird. "Why would anyone want to be friends with such an awkward person? What if I say something stupid?" He thought. "Better to be invisible than show everyone what a fool I am."

He'd still never been in a relationship or even kissed someone. He felt different from everyone else, like there was something wrong with him. How would he ever get a job? Get married? Get through life?

During his first meeting with a counselor, Jack learned about social anxiety disorder and cognitive behavioral therapy. Together they worked on identifying thoughts that Jack had when he was in anxiety-provoking situations and how these contributed to his anxiety and feeling bad about himself. He learned that he tended to think the worst—that everyone was constantly judging him and that he never measured up. It gradually became clear to Jack how these thoughts were contributing to the way he felt.

Types of Anxious Thoughts

Anxious thoughts tend to follow predictable patterns. Most common among these patterns are those that anticipate something bad happening in the future, those that involve self-criticism, and those that reflect a feeling of hopelessness. Let's have a look at examples of each of these types of anxious thoughts.

WHAT IF?

Jack spent a lot of time worrying about what might happen. "What if I say the wrong thing?" he would think when speaking to a classmate. "What if everyone can see how anxious I am when I give a presentation?"

Many of our anxious thoughts come in the form of "what if" statements. "What if that dog attacks me?" "What if my health fails?" "What if my hands start to shake when I am at dinner?" "What if I have a panic attack when I am in that elevator?"

As you can see, these statements usually involve jumping to some sort of conclusion about what could happen in the future and imagining that the worst will happen. We call this "catastrophizing," or the act of blowing things out of proportion.

This type of worrying can also involve mind reading or believing that you know what other people are thinking. This is particularly true for social anxiety disorder. You probably do a lot of predicting—about bad things that could happen in the future and how people will react to them.

You might also make predictions about what feelings in your body mean. This last point is particularly true if you have panic disorder—you probably think that if you feel anxious, it must mean there is something to be feared. However, feelings can have many causes and do not always reflect reality.

Do you have a lot of "what if" thoughts? Write down some that are common for you.

_____

_____

_____

_____

_____

_____

_____

_____

_____

THE CRITIC

Jack was also very critical of himself. When he talked to other people, there was always a running commentary in his mind saying things like "You are so boring," "Nobody likes you," or "You always screw up."

Anxiety can lead you to have thoughts that incorporate criticism or a need for perfection. You review situations that have happened, only focus on what went wrong, and ignore everything that went right.

Thoughts along these lines usually go something like "That was stupid," or "I have to do everything right." You see things as black and white, good or bad, right or wrong. If you spill a drink at a party, it means that the whole situation is ruined, that you have messed everything up, and that you'll never be invited back again.

Along with perfectionism comes personalizing—placing blame on yourself for external events that are outside of your control. If you have generalized anxiety disorder, you probably have trouble living with uncertainty and may feel that you must do everything possible to ensure a good outcome. If something bad does happen, you feel responsible—as if you could have gone one step further to prevent it from happening.

What kinds of critical thoughts do you have about yourself? Identify a few of these and write them in the space below.

_____

_____

_____

_____

_____

_____

_____

_____

_____

_____

_____

_____

_____

"Striving for excellence motivates you; striving for perfection is demoralizing."
—psychologist Harriet Braiker

PLAYING THE VICTIM

Jack had a habit of thinking like a victim. He felt like he could not cope with social situations that were easy for other people and that his anxiety would always be a problem. "I can't cope with presentations" and "I will always be a bad conversationalist" were common thoughts for him.

If you live with anxiety, you probably have thoughts about not feeling capable. Your thoughts may be along the lines of "I can't cope with other people not liking me," or "I can't leave the house alone, I won't be able to manage if I start to panic."

Often this takes the form of overgeneralizing—turning one event into a larger problem. You might think, "If I am late for work, I will fail at my job." As another example, one bad encounter with a dog would mean to you that all dogs must be feared.

Overgeneralizing can also sometimes involve giving yourself labels. You might call yourself "weird," "strange," or "boring" because of your social awkwardness, while ignoring all of your positive traits.

What thoughts do you have that involve a feeling of not being able to cope? Write some of these in the space below.

_____

_____

_____

_____

_____

_____

_____

_____

SOCIAL SKILLS TRAINING

If you have social anxiety, you may benefit from another form of help called social skills training (SST). This can be useful if you have not had a lot of opportunity to practice social interactions or lack people skills.

Social skills training usually starts with an assessment of your skill deficits. SST techniques include the following:

Instruction. The therapist models appropriate behaviors or describes skills and how to carry them out. For example, your therapist would explain that a conversation involves making an introduction, finding something in common to talk about, and then excusing yourself when you leave.

Role-playing. Role-play involves practicing new skills during simulated situations with a therapist. For example, you might practice calling someone on the telephone during a role-play. Role-play gives you the opportunity to practice skills in a safe environment before trying them out in real-life situations.

Feedback and reinforcement. During this part of SST, your therapist will tell you how you are doing and praise any improvements that you make. This helps you stay motivated to develop social skills if anxiety is holding you back.

Homework. Just as with CBT, you will be assigned homework during SST to practice new skills you learn in real-life situations. Applying what you learn in this way helps you master and retain these new skills.

How Thoughts Cause Anxiety

We've identified some of the unhelpful thoughts that you've been having. Next, let's consider how these thoughts can lead to anxiety.

Although it probably seems as though situations cause your anxiety, such as giving presentations, being around feared objects or situations, or facing stressful life situations, these things can't directly cause your physical experience of anxiety. In fact, your thoughts are the link between a situation and your anxious reaction.

"Hi, I'm Seth." A red-haired guy with a wide smile sits down beside Jack and extends his hand. Jack fumbles a bit, shifts awkwardly in his seat, and then weakly offers a handshake. "I'm Jack," he says too quietly, afraid to look the classmate in the eye. "What do you think of this class?" Seth asks easily, still smiling. Jack feels the heat rising to his cheeks and his breath becomes shallow. His heart starts to pound so loudly in his chest that he is sure everyone can hear it. "It's all right, I guess," he says quietly, still looking down at the floor. He starts counting floor tiles and hopes Seth gives up soon.

In this interaction, it seems to Jack as though his anxious symptoms and behaviors arise directly from talking to Seth.

Jack's therapist, however, suggests that there must be a missing piece of this puzzle. What sorts of thoughts, attitudes, perceptions, and expectations did he have when Seth was talking to him? How did they affect his reaction?

Jack admits to thinking that Seth was only talking to him out of pity. He thought Seth would eventually notice his anxiety, think he was weird, and decide to move on to someone else. He also admitted to talking quietly and giving one-word answers so that Seth would not see how anxious he was.

In this way, they created a new understanding of what happened.

THOUGHT(S)

Think I will be judged negatively

EVENT

Stranger talks to me

EMOTION(S)

Can't breathe, heart pounds, talk quietly, look away

Identifying Your Thoughts

Think of a recent situation in which you felt strong anxiety. Perhaps you identified one in your Worry Diary that you can use here as an example.

What event did you identify? Think about it as vividly as you can. Who was there, where were you, what time of day was it? Events can be situations, but they may also be thoughts or memories.

Then, think about the consequences of the situation in terms of your feelings and behaviors. What feelings did you have and what actions did you take? Write down your thoughts in the space below. Choose the one feeling or emotion that seemed the strongest in relation to the event and circle it.

_____

_____

_____

_____

_____

_____

Now take a moment to dig down and identify the thoughts, attitudes, perceptions, or expectations that you had during this situation. If you have a hard time identifying your thoughts, consider what kind of thoughts could have led to the feelings you had. Take a moment and record these below. Choose the one that bothers you the most and circle it.

_____

_____

_____

_____

_____

_____

Now, using the diagram below, write in the event, the thought that you circled, and the feeling that you circled.

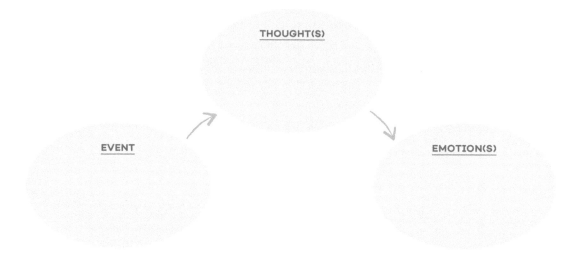

THOUGHT(S)

EVENT

EMOTION(S)

The types of thoughts that contribute to your anxiety will vary depending on the type of anxiety you experience. In the following sections, I describe common types of thoughts related to different kinds of anxiety. Choose the sections that apply to you and practice identifying thoughts that contribute to your anxiety.

Common Thought Patterns

Just as there are common patterns of anxious thoughts, there are also predictable patterns of the types of thoughts you have depending on your specific anxiety. The following sections describe some typical thought patterns for each of the anxiety disorders that we have discussed. Depending on your specific anxiety symptoms, you may wish to focus only on the sections that apply to you.

SPECIFIC PHOBIA

Individuals with specific phobias engage in unhelpful thinking patterns that contribute to their anxiety. If you fear flying, you might overestimate the likelihood of a plane crashing and be vigilant for signs of mechanical failure. If you have a spider phobia, you might overestimate the likelihood and consequences of being bitten. Claustrophobia could cause you to doubt your ability to cope with being in an enclosed space. Thoughts in specific phobia usually center around "what if" scenarios.

Some examples of thoughts in specific phobia include the following:

- What if the elevator cables break and the elevator crashes?

- What if I lose control and throw myself off this cliff?

- What if the snake gets out of its enclosure and bites me?

Think of a recent situation in which you felt fear or anxiety. Identify thoughts that you had that may have contributed to your anxiety. In the diagram below, write down the situation the main thought you had, and the emotion you experienced.

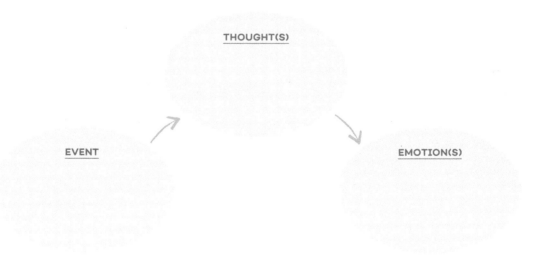

THOUGHT(S)

EVENT

EMOTION(S)

GENERALIZED ANXIETY DISORDER

If you have GAD you may feel that you worry all day every day and overestimate the likelihood of the worst happening. This worry probably applies to all areas of your life, including family, finances, career, health, and relationships. You probably have "what if" thoughts and are critical of yourself or feel unable to cope.

You might have thoughts like the following:

- What if I get in an accident?

- What if I can't handle this new job?

- What if I am diagnosed with a terrible disease?

- What if I go bankrupt?

- If I don't get a perfect job review, I will lose my job.

- I must always make sure that things go smoothly.

- I need to consider all possibilities so I can ensure a good outcome.

You may even worry about your worrying. You might think that too much worrying will make you crazy. On the other hand, you could feel anxious about giving up your worry, as though it is protecting you in some way. You probably have trouble tolerating uncertainty, and worry may feel productive to you—as though you are working on fixing what is wrong.

If you have GAD, you may have a hard time identifying the specific situations that trigger your anxiety, because it seems to be constant. This is where your Worry Diary will come in handy.

Look back and see if you were able to pinpoint specific situations in which you felt more worried than usual. What preceded your episodes of intense anxiety? Were you leaving to drive on the freeway to work? Faced with the possibility of a promotion to a position with more responsibility? Waiting in the doctor's office? Paying your bills?

Try to identify thoughts you had that may have contributed to your anxiety. In the diagram below, write down the event, thoughts, and emotions that you had.

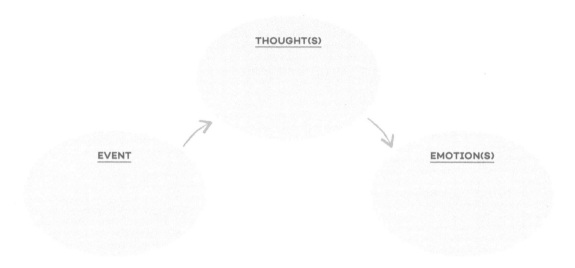

SOCIAL ANXIETY DISORDER

Jack eventually got a job working as a research assistant on campus. Before and during meetings with other students, he found himself becoming very anxious. His mind would go blank when asked a question and his hands would shake when he tried to take notes. He often barely said a word and let others do all the talking.

Jack's counselor helped him identify the thoughts that connected the situation (being in a meeting) to his anxious symptoms.

"What were you feeling in that meeting today?" asked the counselor.

Jack thought for a moment. "I was worried about making a mistake in front of everyone. That they would think I was strange or weird because I was so nervous." He thought some more. "I guess I felt like if I didn't do everything perfectly, the whole meeting was a failure."

Thoughts that trigger social anxiety center around being judged by others or feeling like others may notice your anxiety. Though it may feel as though a situation directly causes your racing heart, shaking hands, and blank mind, it's the thoughts you have about the situation that cause your reaction.

When it came to public speaking, Jack had thoughts such as, "Everyone will see how nervous I am," "I won't be able to stop my hands from shaking," and "People will be bored."

In general, you might have thoughts like the following:

- I haven't said anything in a long time. Everyone must think I am strange.

- Nobody is talking to me. They must not like me.

- When I walk in a room, I can feel everyone staring at me.

- I always do things wrong. I am always making mistakes in front of people.

- Everyone thinks I am a bad public speaker. I get so nervous I am sure they can tell.

Go back to your Worry Diary (page 50) and identify a situation in which you felt anxious. Now, identify the thoughts you had at the time that may have contributed to how you felt. Write down the event, your thoughts, and the emotional outcome in the spaces below.

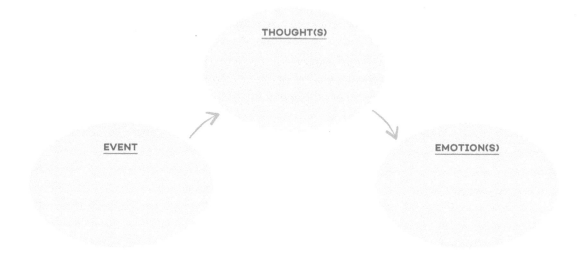

THOUGHT(S)

EVENT

EMOTION(S)

PANIC DISORDER

If you have panic disorder, you likely engage in catastrophic thinking—during which the "what if" questions start to spin out of control. You may worry that your anxiety symptoms mean there is something physically wrong with you and may also worry that others will notice you having a panic attack in public.

Below are some examples of anxious thoughts in panic disorder:

- I feel like I am going to die or go crazy.

- I should always be in control. I can't let anyone see me panic.

- My heart is beating so fast, I must be having a heart attack.

- I feel so dizzy and light-headed. I think I am going to faint.

Go back to your Worry Diary (page 50) and have a look at the situations that triggered your panic. Can you identify any thoughts you were having at the time? Write down the situation, and your main thought and reaction in the spaces below.

AGORAPHOBIA

Agoraphobia involves the fear of having a panic attack somewhere that other people will notice or from which it will be hard to escape. Along these lines, thoughts that perpetuate this type of anxiety include those of worrying what would happen if you had a panic attack in public.

Below are two examples of these types of thoughts.

- What if I lose control and have a panic attack in public where others can see?

- I won't be able to get out of here if I start to have a panic attack.

Go back to your Worry Diary (page 50). Can you identify a situation that triggered feelings of panic related to agoraphobia? Write down the situation, your main thought, and the outcome.

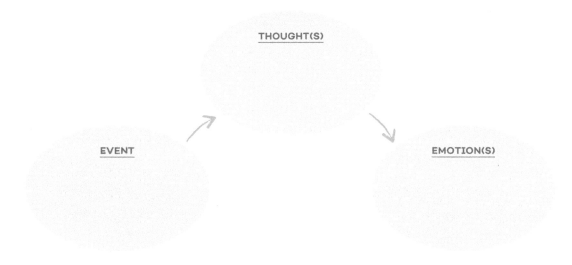

It might seem contradictory that people with agoraphobia fear both open and closed spaces. In fact, they fear situations from which it would be difficult for them to escape or get help if things went wrong. The key fear is that they won't be able to get help or get somewhere safe if they start to panic.

Revealing Your Core Beliefs

When Jack looked at all the thoughts he and his counselor had identified, he began to see a pattern. The emerging theme was that he thought that he was not good enough. This encompassed his feelings that he was socially inept and a poor public speaker, that he dressed inappropriately, that other people noticed his anxiety, and that people thought he was boring and awkward. Jack acknowledged that this core belief described him well—a feeling of never measuring up in the eyes of others.

JACK'S CORE BELIEF DIAGRAM

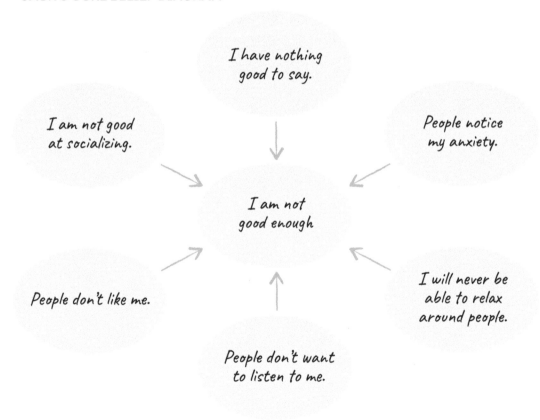

The process of identifying your core beliefs is not much different from what you have already been doing. It involves extending the thoughts that you have identified out to their common theme. One way to get at these core beliefs is to ask yourself, "What does that mean?" in response to your negative thoughts.

For example, Jack's counselor asked him what it meant if he was not good at socializing. Jack replied that it meant people would not like him. His therapist asked again, what it meant if people did not like him. Jack replied that there must be something wrong with him. That he was not good enough.

Your core belief is the big fear that drives your other fears. Your other fears also feed back into it and give it strength. If you are like Jack and believe that you are not good enough, thoughts of people not liking you fit within that core belief.

If you find yourself worrying a lot about bad things that could happen in the future, shift your focus to the present moment. Take a deep breath and look at the world around you. What do you see? Hear? Smell? Focusing on the present will help you move away from anxious thoughts.

Thought Diary

This week I would like you to complete the Worry Diary (page 50) again for at least three events that result in you feeling anxious. For each event, please also complete the Identifying Thoughts (pages 59–60) form to narrow down the thought that came between the situation and how you were feeling. Try to do this as soon as possible after the event, so that you can easily remember what you were thinking.

JEN'S FEAR OF MAKING INTRODUCTIONS

Jen meets with her therapist about her fear of making introductions when meeting new people. Below is what transpired in one of her therapy sessions as they worked together to get at the beliefs that lay underneath Jen's fear and behavior.

> **Jen:** *I feel too nervous to introduce myself to people. I feel like I will do it wrong and so I say nothing. Then they probably end up thinking I am stuck up or aloof.*

> **Therapist:** *So, you are worried that other people will see how bad you are at making introductions? What is bad about that?*

> **Jen:** *I guess I just feel like I will make a fool of myself or embarrass myself.*

> **Therapist:** *And what would be bad about that?*

> **Jen:** *I would feel stupid and like I wanted to escape from the situation. It would just ruin the whole thing.*

Jen and her therapist went on to identify the kinds of things she was telling herself in social situations. They phrased these as "must" statements. Each of these could be considered core beliefs that she held.

- I must come across well to others or I am worthless.

- I must do well in social situations or I am no good.

- I must not make mistakes in social situations or it means there is something wrong with me.

Although you won't be working with a therapist in this program, you can use the same processes to identify your core beliefs on your own. Start with your worry about a situation that causes you anxiety, and ask yourself the question: "What would be bad about that?" to get at the deeper beliefs underlying your anxiety.

Tracking Your Progress

I've also included an optional tool for you to track your progress over the coming weeks of this program. This tool requires you to answer four questions about how you are feeling now in relation to when you started this journey. Each week, you can plot your progress, so that you have a visual representation of how are you are doing. If you wish to use this tool, find the Tracking Your Progress chart at the back of the book (see page 187), and follow the instructions provided there.

Review and Reflect

In this chapter, we've discussed your thoughts and how they contribute to your anxiety. We also looked at the process of identifying core beliefs and how they make your anxiety worse. In the next week, we will spend more time identifying and challenging your core beliefs. Make a commitment to come back for week 3 and plan a time to do so.

How are you feeling so far? This process can be a lot of work, especially if you are not used to actively monitoring your thoughts. However, I encourage you to stick with it. Becoming aware of your thoughts takes time and is a skill that can be learned. Gradually, it will become more of an automatic process.

Now is also a good time to check in with yourself. Write down anything that you are thinking in relation to what you've read this week.

_____

_____

_____

_____

_____

_____

_____

_____

_____

_____

_____

_____

ACTIVITY PLAN

1. Complete the Worry Diary (page 50) for at least three situations.

2. Complete the Tracking Your Progress chart at the back of the book (page 187).

3. Schedule a time to return for week 3.

Breaking Away from Negative Thought Patterns

Last week we identified negative thoughts that contribute to your anxiety and made a plan to practice identifying these thoughts using your Worry Diary and the Identifying Thoughts form. At the end of the last chapter, we also began to explore the concept of core beliefs—the main themes at the core of your negative thoughts that are also reinforced by them. In this chapter, we will identify your own core beliefs and learn how to break your negative thought patterns.

Lola's Fear of Heights

Lola remembers first feeling a fear of heights when she and a friend were vacationing in Mexico. Their condo overlooked the ocean from the 21st floor and had a sliding patio door with a small balcony. Lola remembers stepping out onto the balcony and looking down at the railing and floors below her. She suddenly became aware of danger—that the railing might give way and she could fall, or worse—that she would suddenly lose control and jump to her death.

After that incident, Lola felt very anxious going to high floors of buildings and could not go out on high balconies without starting to panic. Bridges she used to cross often suddenly seemed frightening, and even climbing a small stepladder at home was difficult. Then, at a conference in Chicago, colleagues invited her to visit the famous Hancock building and take in the view of Lake Michigan from 1,000 feet. "I'm not feeling well; I think I'll stay behind," she told them, too embarrassed to talk about her fear. It was then she felt that she needed to get help.

Lola's therapist confirmed that she had a phobia of heights that likely began when she was in Mexico. Her therapist explained that her thoughts in those situations—what if I fall, what if I jump, heights are not safe—were worsening her anxiety and causing her to panic. Together they began to work on a plan for Lola to overcome her fear and move forward in her life.

This week we are going to examine your thoughts and question their accuracy. At this point, I'd like you to go back to your Worry Diary and Identifying Thoughts forms (pages 50 and 59) from last week. Choose one situation and write down the thoughts you identified in the space below. As we work through this chapter, we will analyze these thoughts and see how well they hold up to scrutiny.

_____

_____

_____

_____

_____

_____

_____

"If you gathered up all the fearful thoughts that exist in the mind of the average person, looked at them objectively, and tried to decide just how much good they provided that person, you would see that not some but all fearful thoughts are useless. They do no good. Zero. They interfere with dreams, hopes, desire, and progress." —Richard Carlson

Why Do We Hold on to Beliefs?

As much as she tried, Lola could not shake her phobia of heights. She was convinced something bad would happen and that it would be naive or overly optimistic for her to think otherwise. She was always listening for stories that confirmed her fears, such as the toddler on the news who tumbled off a second-story balcony. In her mind, changing her beliefs would require a significant shift in perspective.

As you work on analyzing your thoughts and beliefs, you will likely encounter roadblocks to letting go of those that turn out to be false or unhelpful. In general, there are three reasons why you may cling to unhelpful or false beliefs:

First, like Lola, you might think there is truth to what you believe and that letting go of that belief would be a superficial way to address your problem. You feel the need to be convinced that your belief is false, and so far, you have not seen evidence in support of that theory.

Second, you might know on a logical level that your belief is false, but it still affects you in an emotional way. For example, you might know on some level that trying to achieve perfection in every social situation isn't rational, but the thought persists and causes you distress.

Finally, beliefs are sometimes maintained simply out of habit. You know that your belief is false and it no longer has a strong influence on your emotions—but you still can't let it go. These beliefs are like a broken record playing background music in your mind. For example, if you have panic disorder, you might logically know that your symptoms do not mean you are having a heart attack, but the thought still presents itself every time.

Think about your own situation. Do you hold on to thoughts because you believe strongly they are true? Are there some thoughts that you no longer fully believe, but still cause you distress? Do you have anxious thoughts that are just bad habits? Look back on the thoughts that you recorded in the previous section, and consider why you are holding on to them. Record your observations below.

_____

_____

_____

_____

_____

_____

_____

_____

_____

_____

_____

_____

_____

_____

_____

_____

_____

SIX QUICK WAYS TO MANAGE NEGATIVE THINKING

A technique known as "thought stopping," which involves snapping a rubber band or taking some other action each time you have a negative thought, has garnered some interest over the years. The logic behind this technique is that you can train yourself to stop having negative thoughts.

Unfortunately, it may do the opposite and lead to increased negative thinking, as you constantly remain vigilant for errant thoughts. Your goal should not be to eliminate all negative thoughts, but rather learn to manage them better. Like annoying pop-up advertisements on many websites, negative thoughts will always arise—but you don't need to give them your attention. Below are six simple ways to manage your negative thinking in the moment.

1. **Just a thought.** Label your thought as just a thought and not a fact. For example, tell yourself, "I am having the thought that I am afraid to give this presentation to my colleagues." This helps to distance yourself and be more objective.

2. **Reduce a thought's power.** Imagine saying your thought in a funny voice or singing it to the tune of a children's song. Your thought will seem absurd in this context and its power will be reduced.

3. **Be proactive.** Counteract your negative thought in a proactive way. If you are worried about failing at your job, make a list of your accomplishments at work.

4. **Evaluate the thought.** Ask yourself, "Is this thought true, important, or helpful?" Identifying thoughts as unhelpful will allow you to distance yourself from them.

5. **Detach from the thought.** Imagine yourself writing the thought on a piece of paper and sending it away as a message in a bottle. Watch as the thought floats away from you.

6. **Set aside a time to worry.** Set aside a time in the future to deal with worrying thoughts so that you can let go of them in the present.

Challenging Negative Thinking

Lola still believed that the thoughts she had about heights were true. She was sure there was actual danger in those situations and it was going to take a lot to convince her otherwise. Lola's therapist had her keep track of events that triggered her anxiety and thoughts that she remembered having in those situations. Lola looked back at her notes from the previous week and chose one that stood out to her.

"I was hiking with my friend on a trail in a conservation area near my house. We got to the end of the trail, and there was a tall cliff overlooking the lake with a chain-link fence. My friend walked right over to it like it was nothing at all. Meanwhile, I felt like racing back down the trail to safety. I was frozen in place about 20 feet away from the edge. I couldn't even look at her, my heart was pounding so fast," Lola said, describing what happened.

"I see the thought you've underlined as most distressing is 'The cliff was dangerous,'" her therapist commented.

"Well, yes," Lola said. "It was so high, imagine if I had fallen! I was terribly worried about my friend, but she seemed not to be fazed by it at all."

Her therapist then suggested that the two of them examine this thought carefully and the evidence for and against it.

"What evidence is there to support your thought that the cliff was dangerous?" her therapist asked.

Lola thought for a moment. "Well, I have heard stories of people who slipped and fell down cliffs and became very injured or even died," she said.

Together they considered any evidence that did not support her thought. "I suppose, since the fence was there, it would have been impossible for me to actually fall down the cliff," Lola noted. "I know many people visit this park and I've never heard of anyone falling off this cliff. I don't imagine a trail would have been built there if it was really unsafe." Together they identified several factors that seemed to contradict Lola's thought that the cliff was dangerous.

EVIDENCE FOR MY THOUGHT	EVIDENCE AGAINST MY THOUGHT
• People can become injured or die from falling off cliffs.	• Most public places near cliffs have safety precautions like guardrails or fences. • Falls from high cliffs are not very common. • People who are cautious and don't take risks are unlikely to fall from cliffs.

Lola's therapist had her reassess her original thought. "I guess it's not really that accurate," Lola said.

"What makes it inaccurate?" Lola's therapist pressed her further.

"Realistically, that cliff was reasonably safe. I was being cautious and there was a fence along the edge."

Together, Lola and her therapist worked on devising a new thought that took into account a more balanced perspective of the situation.

"Cliffs can be dangerous, but it's safe to approach this one with caution."

Between the two thoughts, Lola remarked that the first one seemed a bit alarmist while the second was more realistic and helpful. She paused for a long time before saying, "I can see how the first thought had me paralyzed. Panic would be the natural reaction to that thought. The second thought sounds more rational. If I had to go to that cliff with two people, I would want to go with the person who had the realistic frame of mind. That person seems more clear headed." Lola had recognized the emotional charge of her unhelpful thought and how it was affecting her.

Now I would like you to think about the situation you identified earlier in this chapter. Choose the one thought that seemed to cause you the most anxiety in that situation—we consider this the "hot" thought or the one that triggers your emotional reaction. Then use the Challenging Your Thoughts form below to identify evidence for and against your thought, evaluate the accuracy of your thought, and come up with a more realistic alternative.

Below are some questions to ask yourself when filling out the form:

- Are you certain that your thought is true?

- Looking objectively at your life experiences, what evidence is there to support your thought?

- What evidence is there that the opposite is true?

- Are you overestimating the danger?

- Is there a different explanation?

- Does your thought take into account the whole picture?

EVIDENCE FOR MY THOUGHT	EVIDENCE AGAINST MY THOUGHT

WHEN THOUGHTS ARE ACCURATE

Lola and her therapist determined that the thoughts underlying her height phobia were not realistic and that she was overestimating danger in these situations. Of course, accidents do happen and bad outcomes result, but the likelihood of it happening in Lola's case was so small that her anxiety was out of proportion to the situation. Often in the case of specific phobias, you fear something that is unlikely to happen. Since there is not sufficient evidence to support your belief, it can instead be replaced with a more realistic interpretation. This is true if you have a fear of flying, for example, because the actual risk of a plane crashing is very low.

Now let's consider more general types of anxiety. Are there instances when thoughts and beliefs may be accurate? Perhaps you think that your hands will shake while eating dinner at a restaurant with friends. In examining the evidence, you might find that in the past, your hands quite often shook in this type of situation. It seems that your thought is accurate in this case—the likelihood that your hands will shake is probably high. Ask yourself, what is the worst-case scenario if my thought is accurate? If you accept that your hands are going to shake a bit when out at a restaurant, but realize that it's not a catastrophe if it happens, then that thought loses some of its power.

In situations like this, you will probably find that the outcomes you expect are not as bad as you fear. If your emotional reaction to them happening is out of proportion to the event, it could be that the thought reinforces a core belief that is inaccurate. In this case, your core belief might be that you must never show anxiety in the company of other people.

Think about your own situation. Are you fearful of events that have an extremely low probability of happening? If you fear events that are likely to happen, is the outcome a disaster or could you find a way to cope with it? Write down your thoughts in the space below.

_____

_____

_____

_____

_____

_____

_____

_____

_____

_____

_____

_____

_____

_____

_____

_____

The way in which we perceive events, situations, and what other people say and do is directly related to our own experiences. These experiences create beliefs about ourselves, others, and the world. In this way, our core belief system is what helps us make sense of what we experience. When your core beliefs are negative, altering them can be the catalyst for long-lasting, positive change.

Changing Core Beliefs

The goal of challenging Lola's thoughts was not for her to blindly engage in positive thinking. Instead, she and her therapist worked toward a more realistic and helpful appraisal of the situations that she feared. Unhelpful thoughts often involve a false appraisal of a situation, which can lead to heightened anxiety. The next step was for Lola and her therapist to identify the core belief at the root of her negative thoughts.

"So, what does it mean if that cliff was dangerous?" Her therapist asked. "So what?"

Lola looked at her a bit puzzled. "Well, it was very frightening for me. I thought I might die. I was panicking but I tried not to show it."

Her therapist pressed further. "Why not? What would be bad about showing you were afraid?"

Lola thought again. "It would mean there was something wrong with me. My friend would think I had gone crazy."

Together they completed the Core Belief diagram for Lola and identified the negative thoughts she had about heights that connected to her core belief that she would lose control in the situation.

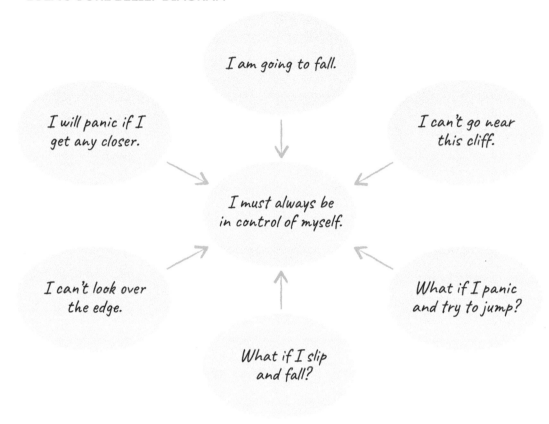

DEVELOPING ALTERNATIVES

Lola was relieved that her phobia could be overcome. The next time she and her friend took the trail near the cliff, she stopped for a moment and stood at the fence. The thought, "This is dangerous, I am going to panic," floated briefly into her mind, but she recognized it and quickly replaced it with the more realistic alternative, "This is safe, as long as I am cautious." She forced herself to stop for a moment to take in the scenery she'd been missing. The water on the lake was calm with only a few ripples. The cattails and evergreens framed the lookout point. "How beautiful," she thought. "I wonder what else I've been missing."

Now I'd like you to complete a Core Belief diagram for your own situation. Identify a core belief and the supporting negative thoughts that have maintained or grown out of that core belief. You may even have multiple core beliefs that are maintained by different sets of thoughts. Complete as many of the Core Belief diagrams as necessary to identify the main themes of your negative thinking. If you're having trouble getting to the core, ask yourself questions about your negative thoughts, such as "What does that mean?" or "What would be bad about that?"

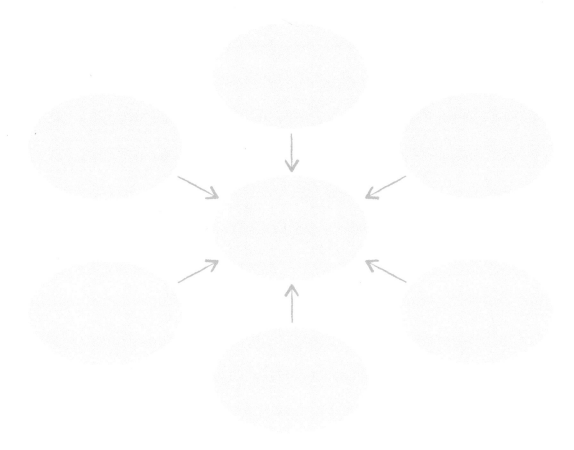

Core beliefs are maintained because of something called "confirmation bias." We tend to look for evidence that confirms our beliefs and discount evidence that is contrary to them. In the space below, I would like you to write down the core belief that you would most like to challenge. Then consider any experiences that you've had that are counter to your core belief.

For example, if your core belief is that you are worthless, you might write things such as "I am a devoted parent," or "I volunteer my time." Based on the facts that run counter to your belief, generate a new more balanced and realistic belief. What would you tell someone else in the same position as you? For example, your new alternative belief might be "I am a worthwhile person."

_____

_____

_____

_____

_____

_____

_____

_____

_____

_____

_____

_____

"The greatest weapon against our stress is our ability to choose one thought over another." —William James, American philosopher and psychologist

USING POSITIVE AFFIRMATIONS

Positive affirmations can be used to challenge your unhelpful or inaccurate core beliefs. Affirmations are short statements that you repeat to yourself either in writing or verbally. Below are some tips for writing positive affirmations and putting them to use.

Keep positive affirmations short. Short, simple affirmations that are in the present tense work best. This makes them easier to remember and indicates change in the present rather than at some point in the future. Saying "I am calm" is better than "I have the ability to stay calm even during stressful situations," or "I will stay calm."

Use positive words. "I remain calm when speaking to strangers" is better than "I am not afraid when speaking to strangers." Fearful language has a way of sticking with you even when phrased negatively, so it's wise to use positive words.

Be realistic. The best affirmations are about changes you want to see in your life and that you are willing to work toward, such as "I am a confident public speaker," or "I am learning to become a confident public speaker."

Remind yourself. Write down your affirmations in a diary each morning or put them on sticky notes in places you will see each day, such as your bathroom mirror or computer monitor.

Make a recording. Record yourself reading the affirmations. Leave 5 to 10 seconds between each affirmation so that you have time to slowly process what you hear. Listen to this recording once a day for a month. Listen while cleaning the house, driving your car, or before falling asleep.

Keep a log. At the end of each day, write down events from the day that confirmed your affirmations. This will help to strengthen your new belief.

While at first it may feel uncomfortable or awkward to say things about yourself that you don't quite believe, with time it should become more natural. It's much like the old saying "fake it till you make it." The same can be true for how you talk to yourself.

Common Core Beliefs

Core beliefs reflect what you think about yourself, others, and the world around you. They are the sum of your negative thoughts and are influenced by your experiences, childhood upbringing, culture, values, faith, and current circumstances. Often core beliefs have themes of being helpless, unlovable, or worthless. They usually follow the format "I am" or "I must." Below are some common core beliefs for each type of anxiety. You can skip over the sections that don't relate to the type of anxiety that you experience.

SPECIFIC PHOBIA

When Lola and her therapist examined her core beliefs, they discovered that she believed she might go crazy or lose control. She was afraid that if she had gone up to the observatory deck in Chicago with her coworkers, she would have lost her mind and done something unpredictable. "How much did you believe that to be true in the situation?" her therapist asked. "One hundred percent," she replied. "That's why I felt I could not go."

If you panic when faced with a snake, dog, needle, high place, or other feared object or situation, you may hold a belief that something catastrophic will happen in those situations. Some examples include the following:

- I am going to die.

- I am going to go crazy.

- I am in danger.

- I must always be in control of myself.

If you fear snakes, you might be convinced that you will be bitten and poisoned if you go near one. Claustrophobia might leave you believing that you will panic and go crazy if you ride in an elevator. Core beliefs such as these in specific phobia can be examined for their accuracy. What is the likelihood of a snake being venomous or biting you? How likely is it that riding in an elevator will result in you going crazy?

If you have a specific phobia, think about what core beliefs might be maintaining your negative thoughts. Record your observations in the space below.

_____

_____

_____

_____

_____

_____

_____

_____

_____

SOCIAL ANXIETY DISORDER

A central belief in social anxiety disorder is that you are not good enough. This belief can sometimes develop because of a critical, rejecting, or overprotective parent, or negative experiences with peers.

Some common core beliefs in social anxiety include the following:

- I am worthless (stupid, boring, unlikable, unattractive, undesirable, etc.).

- I don't measure up.

- I am not good enough.

- I must be approved of by other people.

- Other people are judging me.

If you fear talking to strangers, it probably comes from the false belief that you think they will find you boring or unlikable. If you have anxiety about speaking in public, you might feel as though you're not a good enough speaker. In general, any instance in which you find yourself in the company of others may have you feeling that you need to measure up in some way. If your core belief is that you must always have the approval of others, can you turn that around and ask yourself whether that is realistic or helpful?

If you have social anxiety, consider the core beliefs that contribute to your negative thought patterns. Record your observations in the space below.

PANIC DISORDER AND AGORAPHOBIA

I've grouped panic disorder and agoraphobia together because they tend to involve similar core beliefs. Below are some examples of core beliefs that you might have related to panic disorder and agoraphobia:

- I will go crazy.
- I am defective.
- I am helpless.
- I am unable to cope.
- I am vulnerable.
- I must not show weakness.
- I must always be in control.

With panic disorder and agoraphobia, often the core belief is that you must always be in control and not show weakness. Going into public places feels dangerous because of the risk that you will have a panic attack and not be able to escape the situation. If this resonates with you, it may be helpful to question why you feel you must never show vulnerability.

If you have core beliefs related to panic disorder or agoraphobia, write them in the space below.

_____

_____

_____

_____

_____

_____

_____

_____

_____

GENERALIZED ANXIETY DISORDER

Core beliefs in generalized anxiety disorder follow a theme of the world being an unpredictable and dangerous place and a need for control. Unstable childhood environments and parents with overly high expectations can sometimes lay the foundation for these types of core beliefs. Below are some examples of core beliefs in GAD:

- Bad things will happen.

- The world is a dangerous place.

- I must be certain of good outcomes.

With generalized anxiety disorder, core beliefs often are related to a need for certainty when you fear the unknown. It may be helpful in this case to ask yourself similar questions as in specific phobias—what is the likelihood of your fears actually coming true?

Do you identify with any of the types of core beliefs related to generalized anxiety disorder? If so, record your thoughts in the space below.

_____

_____

_____

_____

_____

_____

_____

_____

_____

Putting It All Together

Now that you've identified your negative core beliefs and come up with more realistic alternatives, it is time to start strengthening your new positive core beliefs. Over the next week, I would like you to keep a data log that lists evidence that supports your new core beliefs. For example, if your new belief is "I am confident," you could record the time you shared a contrary opinion during a conversation. Keep a record of these events on the lined pages at the back of this book. Simply note the new belief and then write any instances that support it underneath.

FEAR OF GOING CRAZY OR LOSING CONTROL

A common theme in many anxiety disorders is the fear of going crazy or losing control. For example, you might fear embarrassing yourself or having to be taken away in an ambulance. While anxiety can cause symptoms that make you think you will lose control, this feeling tends to come and go with your level of anxiety. On the other hand, if you were truly losing contact with reality, it's more likely that you would have little awareness of what was happening.

If you find yourself in a situation in which you feel like you are losing contact with the present moment, try focusing on your surroundings. Notice the blue sky, birds chirping, or the smell of someone's perfume—anything that will help bring your focus back to the present.

SELF-SABOTAGE

Over the coming week, be on the lookout for self-sabotage as you work toward challenging your negative thoughts and core beliefs. It can feel frightening letting go of old ways of thinking, and you might find yourself slipping back into old habits, particularly during times of stress. To prevent this from happening, be sure to take moderate steps toward change, take small steps when you feel overwhelmed in situations, and be aware of your own avoidance.

For example, if your tendency in the past was to call a loved one repeatedly for reassurance when your worries overwhelmed you, find alternatives that can also help relieve your stress. Think of what a reasonable person might do in the same situation. If you have a difficult day at work, consider going for a walk or exercising at the gym as an alternative strategy to leaning too much on those around you for reassurance. It's not at all wrong to reach out to loved ones, but avoid doing it repeatedly.

It's important to also be vigilant regarding avoidance as you move toward more positive core beliefs. For example, if you have panic disorder, you might be working on a belief that you are capable of coping with anxious feelings. If this feels overwhelming, you might start to avoid situations you feel could trigger a panic attack. Instead, try to behave as though the core belief were already true. What would you do if you believed you were as capable of coping as others?

Are you concerned that you may fall back into negative thinking and negative core beliefs? Write down any problems you anticipate here and how you will cope if these problems arise.

_____

_____

_____

_____

_____

_____

_____

_____

_____

_____

Review and Reflect

In this chapter, we have worked on challenging your negative thoughts and core beliefs. You've developed more realistic beliefs and made a plan to keep a log of events over the next week that support your new beliefs. By this point we have laid a solid foundation for working on your anxiety. I am excited for the weeks to come, as we take a more hands-on approach and start working on your anxiety in real-life situations. In the coming chapter, we will discuss some roadblocks—like procrastination, panic, and worry—and how to overcome anxiety and deal with them.

I know there's been a lot to take in, and perhaps you are feeling unsure about your ability to translate what you've learned into changes in your life. I suggest focusing on one step at a time, rather than trying to see the finish line. Not only will you feel less apprehensive about what is left to do, but you will also fully engage in each exercise without being overwhelmed.

Now let's take a moment and check in with yourself at this point. How are you feeling about how things are going? Does the plan to alter your beliefs make sense to you? Record your thoughts in the space below.

_____

_____

_____

_____

_____

_____

_____

_____

ACTIVITY PLAN

1. Continue to complete the Worry Diary (page 50) for anxiety-provoking situations.

2. Complete the Challenging Your Thoughts form (page 81) for at least one situation.

3. Keep a data log of events that support your new beliefs in the back of this book.

4. Generate positive affirmations and rehearse them regularly.

5. Complete the Tracking Your Progress chart at the back of the book (page 187).

6. Schedule a time to return for week 4.

Procrastination, Panic, and Worry

Getting Free of Things That Hold You Back

In the previous chapter, we evaluated the accuracy of your negative thoughts. We also examined your negative core beliefs and developed more realistic alternative beliefs. I asked you to continue keeping track of situations that made you anxious, to examine your thoughts in those situations, and to keep a log of events that supported your new beliefs. How did your homework assignments go? Please write down your thoughts about the work you completed last week in the space below.

_____

_____

_____

_____

_____

In this chapter, we will consider three obstacles to overcoming anxiety: procrastination, panic, and worry. These issues tend to be common roadblocks regardless of the type of anxiety you experience. First, let's have a look at how anxiety relates to procrastination and what you can do about it.

Feeling Stuck: Greg's Story

Greg still remembers his first panic attack. He'd always been an anxious person, but that day was like nothing he'd ever experienced. It happened during a football game that he attended with a couple of his good friends. The stadium was full and he found himself tightly wedged between his seatmates.

Out of the blue, Greg began to feel pain in his chest and as though he could not get a full breath of air. "Is this a heart attack?" he remembers thinking. "Am I going to die? It can't end like this." Somehow, he managed to slip through the crowd and out of the stands to the concession area where he spotted a uniformed employee. "Call 911!" He gasped, clutching his chest.

That evening at the hospital, Greg and his family were relieved to learn that they had found no physical cause for his symptoms. At the same time, Greg was confused. He was sure something must be wrong; the doctors had just missed it.

Going forward, Greg developed some unusual behavioral patterns. He would no longer go to sporting events. His wife had to do all the shopping because he refused to go to the store. He still drove his truck to work but took a longer route to make sure he would not be stopped in traffic.

Though he had at one time joked about his tendency to worry, it now consumed him. There had been some layoffs at the factory where he worked, and he constantly feared he was next. He worried that his boys would be injured and found himself constantly monitoring what they did. Money worries also kept him up at night, although they were doing okay financially.

Even his children knew he was not well. "What's wrong with Dad?" their youngest son asked their mother often. After nearly six months, Greg's wife finally insisted he make an appointment with their family doctor.

Greg's doctor referred him to a psychologist who diagnosed him with both panic disorder and generalized anxiety disorder. Greg wasn't sure what to think. On one hand, he was glad to have an explanation, but on the other, he was afraid of what it meant.

Procrastination

We all know what it means to procrastinate. A long to-do list lies in front of you, but instead you find yourself surfing the Internet or emailing a friend. The lawn needs mowing, but the lounge chair on the deck seems much more inviting. I am no stranger to procrastination myself—quite often family and friends have dropped by on the weekend to find my house in a state of disarray, the result of having two active young children and my own distracted attempts to get started tidying up.

As much as he tried, Greg could not get going on tasks in his life. It felt like he didn't know where to start. When he tried to begin a household chore, he found himself stuck mentally working through every possible course of action. He'd been talking about a family camping trip for almost a year. He'd read every guidebook, visited all the websites, even looked up campgrounds to get prices— but he still couldn't move forward with a concrete plan for their vacation.

Do you find yourself procrastinating because of your anxiety? Do you put off making phone calls, take too long to get started on work projects, or fall behind on household chores? Do you struggle with specific tasks or activities? Record your thoughts in the space below.

_____

_____

_____

_____

_____

_____

_____

_____

_____

_____

_____

HOW FEAR HOLDS YOU BACK

Anxiety is a contributing factor to procrastination. When you feel anxious, procrastination can bring about a temporary sense of relief. Unfortunately, procrastination leads to more anxiety, as you fall behind on tasks and pressure mounts. Procrastination resulting from anxiety can be related to a fear of failure or disapproval, it may involve putting off tasks that cause you anxiety in the moment, and it can also just be a bad habit that you have developed.

FEAR OF FAILURE OR DISAPPROVAL

Fear of failure or disapproval closely resembles perfectionism. Do you feel like things should be done in a certain way and question your ability to complete them in this manner? Do you second-guess yourself, feel paralyzed, and avoid taking action for fear you will fail? Do you worry what others will think about what you do? Examples of this type of procrastination include trouble getting started on projects and avoiding tasks that involve social contact.

This type of procrastination is rooted in fear, insecurity, and self-doubt. You might jump to conclusions and think you are not capable of reaching your goals. Thoughts such as "I must complete this task perfectly or not at all," or "I have to get this right, or people will think I am incompetent," may be common for you. However, most of us do not have time for perfection—so tasks end up left undone.

Do you identify with this type of procrastination? Do worry and perfectionism hold you back? Are you afraid to make mistakes? Record your thoughts and some examples below.

_____

_____

_____

_____

_____

_____

_____

_____

_____

_____

INFORMATION OVERLOAD

Anxiety can also lead to procrastination if your working memory is overloaded. If you have trouble concentrating and aren't getting enough sleep, daily activities such as managing finances, tracking children's schedules, or meeting work demands may feel like too much. When your mind is overloaded, it probably feels like everything is too complicated and you don't know where to start.

Are you struggling with information overload? Does every day seem like a struggle and tasks seem too difficult? Record your thoughts below.

_____

_____

_____

_____

_____

_____

_____

_____

_____

_____

INTOLERANCE OF UNCERTAINTY

If you are like Greg, you might procrastinate because you need to feel in control and certain. For example, you might put off making decisions because you don't feel that you have enough information. Then if a deadline eventually looms, you find yourself pressed for time and rushing to make choices. You might even avoid making a decision altogether so that you can't be held responsible for a bad outcome. This type of procrastination is endless—because it never feels like you've done enough.

Do you over-prepare, over-research, or overanalyze? Do you have trouble getting started on tasks because you feel like you still need to gather more information? Are there things you are avoiding doing because you can't be certain of a positive outcome? Record your observations below.

_____

_____

_____

_____

_____

_____

A BAD HABIT

Sometimes, procrastination becomes more of a bad habit than anything—any new task that you're given seems too hard or overwhelming, so your instinct is to delay getting started until you feel more confident or ready. You might even identify yourself as a procrastinator to the point that it becomes part of your personality. In this case, procrastination has become a deep-rooted habit that you need to learn how to break.

Think about your habits and write down any examples of this type of procrastination in your own life in the space below.

_____

_____

_____

_____

_____

_____

OVERCOMING ANXIETY-RELATED PROCRASTINATION

Working through your anxiety using the cognitive behavioral approach is a good first step toward overcoming procrastination. When your fear of disapproval and failure are reduced, you may naturally find it easier to get started on tasks. However, you can also directly address procrastination with some proactive steps.

1. **Make a list and prioritize tasks.** Review your list often and ensure that you are working on the most important tasks. Plan to spend a certain amount of time every day on each high-priority task.

2. **Start somewhere.** If you don't know where to start, break tasks down into small steps. Then complete the first step of a task. If you get stuck on a step because you feel unsure, push yourself to move to the next logical step anyway.

3. **Assess the situation and your expectations.** Give yourself permission to make mistakes. Realistically assess whether perfection is necessary—or even possible. Ask yourself what the best, worst, and most realistic outcome would be if you did not do a task perfectly.

4. **Reward yourself for completing difficult tasks.** When a difficult task on your list is complete, cross it off, and reward yourself with something you find enjoyable.

5. **Use relaxation strategies to cope with anxiety about completing tasks.** We will talk more about relaxation in week 6. Relaxation strategies can be used to calm yourself down and get started on anxiety-provoking work.

6. **Adopt routines and organizational tools.** Don't rely on your mind to keep track of your daily responsibilities—especially if it is already overwhelmed with anxiety. Use tools to keep you organized and on track, such as day planners, file folders for incoming and outgoing correspondence, and apps to keep on top of to-do lists. See the Resources section in the back of this book for more information.

7. **Learn to delegate.** Delegate chores or tasks if you've been doing everything yourself. If you are fearful of things not being done right, use checklists or other systems to ensure tasks are completed to your standards.

8. **Learn by trying.** If you struggle with overanalyzing before taking action, experiment with the idea that taking action is the best way to learn and weigh alternatives.

9. **Don't blame yourself.** Though on the surface, procrastination appears to be a problem of time management, it is often much more complex. Don't blame yourself for being disorganized or lazy, because you aren't. You've simply fallen into some bad habits because of your anxiety.

Do any of the above strategies sound helpful for your situation? Can you identify one task that you would get started on today if you stopped trying to do it perfectly? From the list above, identify which strategies might be helpful to you and record below how you could apply them to your procrastination. Make a to-do list of what you need to get done, and then rank order the list in terms of priority. Schedule time over the next week to work on the highest priority items on your list.

_____

_____

_____

_____

_____

_____

_____

_____

A 2015 study published in the Journal of Behavioral Medicine *demonstrated that people who procrastinate are vulnerable to serious health conditions such as cardiovascular disease and hypertension. Other research has linked chronic procrastination to increased risk of colds, flu, and insomnia. It is thought that putting off tasks causes stress, which increases vulnerability to illness.*

Panic

If you've never experienced a panic attack, you could choose to skip this section. However, you might find learning about panic attacks helpful, as many of the strategies used to manage them can be useful for all types of anxiety.

Greg's psychologist explained that what he'd experienced in the stadium that day was a panic attack.

"What does that mean?" Greg asked. "It felt like a heart attack to me. I've never felt anything like that before."

His therapist nodded. "Yes, it would feel that way at the time. A panic attack is a natural event that occurs out of context. If you'd been facing a threat, such as someone trying to mug you, then your body would have been prepared to fight or run."

Greg looked a bit confused. "But there was nothing wrong. I wasn't in danger."

His therapist nodded again. "Sometimes, panic attacks happen when someone has been under stress for a long time. They can also happen out of the blue, without any kind of warning. During the panic attack, since you don't see anything to be afraid of, you assume that the problem must be inside of you—that you are having a heart attack or some other type of catastrophic experience. Those thoughts in turn cause more fear, anxiety, and panic."

Greg was suddenly quiet. "So you mean it was all an illusion?"

"The symptoms you experienced were very real," his therapist replied, "but the perception of danger was an illusion."

DEFLATING DANGER

During the early stages of a panic attack, you are likely to notice some minor symptoms. However, full-blown panic results only when you perceive and respond to your body in a catastrophic way. One way to gain control over your panic attacks is to reduce your perception of danger. This comes about by understanding that a panic attack is not dangerous in and of itself.

Many of the physical symptoms during a panic attack feel frightening but are not dangerous. While it might feel as though your heart is beating so fast that you will have a heart attack, the heart can sustain a rapid rate over a period of days without any damage. As you breathe more rapidly, blood circulation to your brain is reduced, which could cause you to feel faint. However, the likelihood of you fainting is very low. And even if you were to faint, your brain would eventually force you to breathe if you were not receiving enough oxygen.

If you've experienced panic attacks, I'd like you to take a moment to think about what you felt in those moments. What kind of physical symptoms did you have? Did you have any catastrophic thoughts in the moment that might have made your panic worse? Record your thoughts in the space below.

_____

_____

_____

_____

_____

_____

_____

_____

COPING STRATEGIES

It is possible to learn to cope better with panic attacks. Certain lifestyle changes can make them less likely to occur—or to not feel as intense if they do happen. The work you did in the previous chapter, identifying your core beliefs, will also help you develop a more accepting attitude, which should help reduce your panic.

The key to managing panic attacks is to detect them at an early stage before your symptoms grow out of control. If you recognize symptoms when they first start, then you can use coping strategies to prevent a full-blown panic attack.

Below is a list of strategies for you to try:

1. **Get regular exercise and enough sleep.** Regular exercise will help you manage stress, improve your mood, and release tension. Adequate sleep will also help you think clearly.

2. **Practice relaxation strategies.** Breathing exercises can be used to manage panic in the moment. The following section describes a method to practice deep abdominal breathing.

3. **Cut back on sugar, caffeine, and alcohol, and avoid smoking.** Each of these can make panic attacks worse. Try to avoid them as much as possible.

4. **Acknowledge and express your feelings.** Recognize when you feel angry, sad, frustrated, or worn out. Express these feelings by talking to someone or writing your thoughts in the back section of this book.

5. **Eat well and regularly.** Eating regular healthy meals will help stabilize your blood sugar, which will prevent you from feeling light-headed or dizzy.

6. **Manage stress.** Identify types of stress that make your symptoms worse and find ways to manage them. At the same time, do not restrict your daily activities or avoid situations out of fear of having a panic attack.

7. **Don't fight against or resist symptoms.** This just tends to make them worse. No matter how difficult symptoms feel, try to adopt a practice of accepting them.

8. **Use coping statements.** Repeat a statement to yourself, such as "This is just anxiety." This helps you feel in control rather than a victim of your panic.

9. **Join a support group.** Support groups with others going through the same thing can be helpful so you don't feel alone. Lean on this group for support when you are coping with panic. See the Resources section for suggestions of support groups for different types of anxiety.

Now it's your turn. Take a moment and review the list above. Can you identify any habits that may be contributing to your panic attacks? Are you managing stress and taking care of your physical health? Are you breathing in a way that promotes relaxation? Record your thoughts here about what you are doing right and areas in which you could make improvements.

ABDOMINAL BREATHING

Slow breathing from your abdomen can help alleviate symptoms of panic by slowing your respiratory rate, reducing the constriction of your chest wall muscles, and decreasing symptoms of hyperventilation.

When you feel dizzy or disoriented during a panic attack, it is because you are breathing rapidly from your chest. After three or four minutes of slow abdominal breathing, you should notice your symptoms are reduced. In addition to breathing this way in the moment of panic, you should also practice five minutes each day to train yourself to breathe more deeply on a regular basis.

To practice deep breathing, find a comfortable position. Close your eyes. Notice your breath. Is it shallow from your chest? Are you breathing slowly or quickly?

Now inhale deeply and slowly through your nose and expand your stomach as you breathe. Put your hands on your stomach so that you can see them rise and fall. Gradually, exhale through your mouth, letting out all of the air. If you feel worse during deep breathing, take a break for about 30 minutes and then try again.

If you practice abdominal breathing regularly, it should become natural for you. You will be able to initiate it during a panic attack to cue your body to relax.

Worry

In addition to his panic attacks, Greg dealt with constant worry. His therapist explained to him that his worry was a way of trying to control situations.

"This camping trip that you've been trying to plan. What sort of worries have you had about that?" he asked.

Greg thought for a moment. "Well, I'm worried that the weather could be bad. What if I take a week off work and end up spending it in a tent in the rain?

I'm also worried one of us could get sick while we are away. I need to make sure we're close enough to a hospital just in case. What if one of the boys gets hurt? We need to be close to help. I'm also not sure what to bring. I've tried to think of everything, but every time I start to pack up our gear, I think of something else I've forgotten. What if we get there and I've left something important behind at home?" It seemed easy for Greg to think of what might go wrong on their trip.

"Let me stop you for a minute," Greg's therapist interjected. *"I am hearing about a lot of things that could go wrong. How many of those things are within your control?"*

Greg stopped and thought. *"I guess there isn't much I can do about the weather. Or getting sick. But I do feel responsible for packing what we need and choosing a good location."*

Worry is a central feature of all anxiety disorders. If you have panic disorder, you will worry about when you might have another panic attack. Social anxiety will cause you to worry about what other people think of you. If you have generalized anxiety disorder like Greg, you will worry about all aspects of your life. Though it may feel like you are working on a problem when you worry, it's really not a productive activity that will lead to positive results.

WORTH THE WORRY?

Sometimes we worry about things we can control. Other times, we worry about things that are outside of our control. Worrying can be useful if it leads to you taking action or solving a problem. On the other hand, chronic worry serves no purpose other than to cause you emotional pain. Focusing on worst-case scenarios doesn't make them any less likely to happen—it just causes you additional stress.

Greg was worried about both the weather and choosing the perfect camping location. His therapist helped him identify problems that he could work on versus potential issues that were outside his control.

Take a moment and think about your top worries. Whatever they are, it is likely that some will be within your control, while others will be outside of your control. Ask yourself, is this problem current or a "what if" scenario? If it is a "what if," how likely is it to happen? Is there anything you can do about the problem, or is it outside of your control?

Also consider what you think it means to worry. Do you believe that worrying helps you solve problems? Do you feel that worrying makes you a more conscientious person? Sometimes we find that worrying helps reduce anxiety in the moment because you feel like you are getting something done. However, worrying is not the same as problem solving.

Record some of your worries below, and note whether they are within or outside of your control.

_____

_____

_____

_____

_____

_____

_____

_____

_____

_____

_____

_____

_____

_____

_____

WORRY TRIGGERS

Greg tended to worry late at night. He would like awake in bed, going over all the things that could go wrong in his life. Instead of getting up when he could not sleep, he would toss and turn for hours. He also found that talking with his father made him worry more. His dad was overly cautious just like him and reinforced Greg's belief that he was just one misstep away from misfortune at all times.

Let's take a moment to think specifically about your worrying. When do you tend to worry most? What do you do when you worry? Are there certain people in your life who make your worries worse? Record your thoughts below.

_____

_____

_____

_____

_____

_____

_____

_____

_____

"When I look back on all these worries, I remember the story of the old man who said on his deathbed that he had had a lot of trouble in his life, most of which had never happened." —Winston Churchill

MOVING AWAY FROM WORRY

Just like procrastination, worry is sometimes a bad habit. While the work you have done up to this point changing your negative core beliefs will help you worry less, it will also take some practice to get out of the worry habit.

One way to break the worry habit is to find new habits to replace your worrying. For example, Greg's therapist suggested that he go for a walk if he was worrying during the day or get up and read a book if he found himself tossing and turning at night.

Note that the goal here is not to stop working on the problems that cause you worry. You will always have worries about real-life problems that do need solutions. However, it is better to problem-solve within a defined period than to worry endlessly. You can address your worries during a set time of the day. For now, try your best to let them go.

Have you noticed anything that helps reduce your worry? Do household chores get your mind focused on other things? Would going to the gym break your worry habit? Could watching a funny movie distract you from your worries? Would doing something creative like writing or painting help you move away from your worry habit?

In the space below, come up with five activities that you could do instead of worrying. Try to think of activities that you could do both at home and at work.

1. _____

2. _____

3. _____

4. _____

5. _____

HOW NEGATIVE MOODS FUEL WORRY

Did you know that a negative mood could be making your worry worse? Being in a bad mood can affect what you think about through what is known as the "mood-congruent memory" effect. When you are in a negative or anxious mood, you are more easily able to access negative memories, which trigger even more worrying.

In addition, your negative mood makes you more likely to notice negative things in your environment. For example, you might focus on all the bad news in the media or a disapproving face in a crowd. This effect of your negative mood happens at a level that you are not even consciously aware of.

Negative moods can also cause you to interpret ambiguous situations as negative. For example, you might interpret your supervisor approaching you to mean that he is going to give you bad news.

What's worse, your mood can also determine when you will stop worrying. We tend to go by our mood when deciding if we've worried enough. If you find you're still in a bad mood, then your mind might decide that you must not be done worrying yet.

EXPRESSING YOUR FEELINGS

Sometimes we worry because we are keeping our feelings bottled up. When we worry, we temporarily suppress feelings that we are afraid to experience. In this sense, we are worrying to find a way to express the frustration that we feel.

Is there anyone you can talk to who helps you worry less? Have you tried writing down your thoughts in a journal? Have you ever kept a gratitude journal to balance out your worries? Often we find that our worries grow if we keep them to ourselves. Sharing them with others or expressing them in writing may help you gain perspective.

Take a moment and write down your thoughts about how well you are able to express your feelings. Do you have a confidant or keep a journal? Jot down some ideas that sound helpful for managing your feelings.

_____

_____

_____

_____

_____

_____

_____

_____

_____

_____

"Worry is like a rocking chair: it gives you something to do but never gets you anywhere." —Erma Bombeck

EXAMINING YOUR WORRIES

Greg's therapist suggested that he set aside a time to worry each day. Greg thought this was a bit humorous but agreed to go along with it.

If he found himself worrying at other times of the day, he was instructed to jot down the worry for later consideration. Greg chose to worry from 7:00 to 7:15 p.m. each night at the kitchen table, to give himself time afterward to wind down before bed. His therapist asked him to consult his list of worries during that time and to jot down any potential solutions that he could identify. Then he was asked to transfer any tasks he identified over to his to-do list.

As you think of worries through the day, jot them down in the back of this book (page 192). Then choose a regular time each day to consult this list of worries and generate solutions. Transfer any tasks that you identify need doing over to your to-do list. If you find that some worries on your list are outside of your control, recognize that time spent on them will be wasted.

In the space below, record the time and place each day that you have chosen for reflecting on your worries.

Review and Reflect

This has been a productive week! We've discussed procrastination, panic, and worry, and how they may be related to your anxiety. We've also identified strategies that you can use to reduce their impact on your daily activities. In the coming chapter, we will move on to putting what you've learned so far into practice in real-life situations.

ACTIVITY PLAN

1. Continue to complete the Worry Diary and Challenging Your Thoughts forms (pages 50 and 81).

2. Make a to-do list and apply the procrastination strategies to accomplish your most urgent tasks.

3. Practice deep breathing for five minutes each day.

4. Schedule a worry period each day.

5. Complete the Tracking Your Progress chart at the back of the book (page 187).

6. Schedule a time to return for week 5.

Practicing Behavior

Getting Back to Life and Facing Your Fears

Last week we discussed procrastination, panic, and worry. You continued completing your Worry Diary and Challenging Your Thoughts forms and made a to-do list. In addition, you practiced deep abdominal breathing for five minutes and scheduled a 15- to 20-minute worry period each day. In short, you've made a lot of positive changes in a short period of time. Feel proud of what you have accomplished but don't stop working yet.

Review last week's homework—did any specific situations cause you a lot of anxiety? Were you able to replace your automatic negative thoughts with more realistic alternatives? Write your thoughts below. As we work through this chapter, we will draw on the specific situations that you've recorded.

_____

_____

_____

_____

_____

Procrastination and worry are sneaky feelings and have a way of returning if you are not vigilant. Did you manage to check some items off your to-do list last week? Did you practice deep breathing for five minutes and schedule a worry period each day? If you found this work overwhelming or it was difficult to find time in your schedule, it's okay to set it aside and try again in the coming week. This isn't a race to the finish line—even the smallest steps in the right direction will get you where you need to go. Write down how things went in the space below.

_____

_____

_____

_____

_____

_____

_____

_____

_____

_____

_____

Now, it's time to begin intentionally facing the situations and objects that cause you to experience fear with the aim of reducing the anxiety that you feel in those situations. While in the past, you probably encountered feared situations haphazardly, you will now be engaging in intentional and prolonged exposure to what you fear. If you feel apprehensive, don't worry; we're not going to jump in at a level you can't handle.

Performance Anxiety: Katie's Story

By the time Katie saw a psychologist about her performance anxiety, it had plagued her for nearly a decade. But it hadn't always been that way.

Katie was the youngest of four children. Born to musical parents, she followed in their footsteps and attended a fine arts program after high school. As a young child, Katie was a natural performer. She often put on "recitals" at home and sang to whomever would listen.

Although Katie would become an accomplished pianist and vocalist and grow familiar with performing, she started to struggle through her piano and voice lessons in her teenage years. At times her hands would shake or she would lose her voice while singing.

Because of growing anxiety, Katie channeled her musical ability into teaching instead of performing. After college, she taught music lessons out of a home studio to local children. While she sometimes sang or played the piano during recitals, she was too afraid to audition for local productions.

Katie found that her performance anxiety waxed and waned depending on the audience. She felt relatively confident demonstrating techniques one-on-one to students. However, when she knew that parents would be present for recitals, her anxiety grew to an uncomfortable level.

Katie's anxiety took a turn for the worse during their annual Christmas recital. During a solo performance, she found herself struggling as her voice shook uncontrollably and her throat constricted. Unable to control her anxiety, she rushed to the end of the song. That was the last time she performed a solo during a recital and since then she had been too embarrassed to talk to anyone about what happened.

Over lunch one day with her friend Jane, Katie finally admitted her fears. "I'm afraid of the spotlight. Maybe it's just not for me. I couldn't bear to make a fool of myself again."

Jane was a social worker and a good listener. "Would you be willing to talk with me about your fear?" she asked.

Katie was hesitant. "I don't know. I think I've given up on that chapter of my life."

Jane looked concerned. "Katie, you've faced and overcome so much. Remember how anxious you were teaching your first lesson? You were terrified, but you made it through. I hate to see you give up now."

Something in her friend's words hit home for Katie. She hadn't realized she'd given up her dream of performing. "When did life get so hard?" she wondered. "When did I become so afraid?" She turned to Jane, a bit of sparkle returning to her blue eyes. "Okay, let me know when we can get started."

Even celebrities have performance anxiety. Barbra Streisand forgot the lyrics to a song during a concert in Central Park in 1967 and did not perform live again until 1994. She was treated with both therapy and medication, and continues to use teleprompters to boost her confidence.

What Is Exposure Therapy?

Exposure therapy involves facing what you fear in a safe environment. It can take place *in vivo*, which means in real life, or it can be *imaginal*, which involves vividly imagining what you fear. It can also involve facing bodily sensations that are harmless but that you interpret as dangerous. This is known as *interoceptive exposure*, a CBT technique usually used for panic disorder that involves purposefully inducing a physical symptom that is feared, such as spinning in a chair to create a sensation of dizziness. Finally, virtual reality is becoming popular for facing situations that are difficult to recreate in real life, such as a fear of flying.

Exposure therapy may be graded, in which you develop a fear hierarchy and face fears from least to most difficult. Alternatively, it might involve flooding, where you face the most difficult tasks all at once. Often exposures are combined with relaxation exercises to make them more manageable. We will discuss relaxation next week; if you feel uncomfortable jumping straight into exposures, you could work on these two sections at the same time.

EXPECTING PERFECTION

Katie came to Jane's office the following week. They spent some time talking about Katie's performance fears and thought patterns that contributed to her anxiety. "In that moment, during the recital, what were you telling yourself?" Jane asked.

"That I was no good. That I was messing up badly. There was no going back at that point. Everyone had seen what I'd done. I'd completely ruined it."

Jane nodded. "And how did that make you feel? I can't imagine it made you feel very good."

Katie agreed. "No, it didn't, but I wasn't thinking about that. They were just my thoughts. I couldn't control them."

Jane raised an eyebrow. "Is that true? They were out of your control?"

"It felt that way at the time." Katie sat dejectedly looking out the window. "I am sure you think I could have handled it better."

Jane leaned forward. "I'm not here to judge you, Katie. I want the two of us to look at your thoughts and decide together how they contributed to what happened. Imagine that instead of thinking you'd screwed up, you'd thought you were anxious but could get through it. What might you have felt or done in that moment?"

Katie considered the idea. "Well, I might have relaxed a bit or made a joke about being more nervous than my students. But I didn't . . ." she trailed off.

"Can you think of a belief that might underlie all these thoughts?" Jane asked. "Perhaps that you must never show anxiety while performing?"

Katie nodded. "That would explain why I thought everything was ruined."

"How realistic is it to think that you will never show anxiety?" Jane continued.

Katie thought for a moment. "Not at all. Obviously, we are all human and get anxious sometimes. It's hard to remember that in the moment, though. I can't stop thinking that everyone can see how nervous I am."

"Have you ever been in the audience when a performer seemed anxious?" Jane asked.

"Oh sure," Katie replied. "I remember last year, my friend Matt was in a production of A Midsummer Night's Dream. He completely froze in the middle of a monologue. I remember it was a production in the park. It was a sweltering summer day and we all sat there trying to stay cool. We were waiting for him to speak, and my own heart started to race, I felt so bad for him. Eventually, someone cued him and he got back into the script."

"Did you think he had screwed up the whole play?" Jane asked.

"Of course not! It was just a few moments, and he got over it quickly. By the end, I don't think anyone remembered. We all congratulated him on a successful show."

"Did you congratulate yourself after the Christmas recital?" Jane asked.

"No, but that was different. I was a mess. I completely ruined it for everyone."

"Ruined it for everyone?" Jane looked at her intently. "If Matt had never recovered and walked off the stage, would you have told him he ruined your night?"

"Of course not. I would have felt terribly bad for him. I would have told him it could happen to anyone. Nobody's perfect."

"Nobody?" Jane asked. "Doesn't that include you?"

Through this back and forth discussion, Jane and Katie got to the root of her negative thoughts about performing and her belief that she could not show any anxiety. They generated a more realistic interpretation that matched the kindness she displayed toward her friend.

Can you think of any situations in which you expect too much from your-self? Do you think that everything must go perfectly or you've ruined a situation? Are you kinder toward others than you are toward yourself? Iden-tify any related thoughts and record them below.

_____

_____

_____

_____

_____

_____

_____

_____

_____

Building a Fear Hierarchy

"What we're going to do next," Jane told Katie, "is construct a list of what you fear from least to most anxiety-provoking. After we put this list together, I'll explain more."

"A list?" Katie looked at her questioningly.

"Yes, to start with, I'd like you to name the different performance situations that cause you to feel anxious. Just name them out loud and I'll start writing them down for you," Jane replied.

"Let's see. Obviously, doing a solo vocal causes me to freeze up. Especially in front of a large audience," Katie noted.

"Yes, of course." Jane was writing. "That's probably your biggest fear. Can you think of any related situations that might cause you anxiety? Is there anything you've avoided doing?"

"I've avoided auditioning for local productions. Is that what you mean? I guess that would be my biggest fear, short of performing in one. Recitals are difficult. Even during lessons, I notice lately I feel nervous." With Jane asking questions and Katie answering, together they constructed a list of Katie's performance-related fears.

ACTIVITY	STRESS LEVEL (1–10)
Performing a solo vocal in a local production	10
Performing a solo vocal in a recital	9
Doing a piano solo in a local production	8
Doing a piano solo in a recital	7
Singing with others in a recital	6
Singing for students during one-on-one lessons	5
Piano accompaniment in a local production	5
Piano accompaniment in a recital	4
Piano accompaniment during a one-on-one lesson	4

Now I'd like you to identify a situation you've been avoiding that is important to you. For example, in Katie's case, she had avoided auditioning despite her childhood love of the stage. Below are some examples of situations you might be avoiding:

- Leaving your house
- Riding on public transportation
- Going to the mall
- Riding in an elevator
- Taking a vacation
- Accepting a promotion at work
- Going to a movie theater

- Going to the top floor of a building
- Receiving medical care
- Eating in front of other people
- Talking to strangers
- Using a public restroom
- Being around animals
- Engaging in exercise

Remember, avoidance doesn't necessarily mean that you never face the situation. It can also be subtle, such as not looking at an audience when giving a performance or being careful not to exercise too vigorously. Unless you are fully present in the situation you fear, you are not facing your fear.

It's also important to note that by avoiding some of these situations, such as receiving medical care or accepting a promotion, you may be compromising your health and well-being. In this way, learning to face what you fear may be important to prevent negative impacts in various aspects of your life.

Take a moment and write down a situation that causes you a lot of fear and anxiety: something that is important to you and that you have been avoiding.

_____

_____

_____

_____

Let's imagine you wrote down "going to the mall." If you panic at the thought of going to the mall, it might seem impossible to ever face this fear. Don't worry, we're not going to jump right to your worst fear. This is where the concept of the "fear hierarchy" comes in. Just like you climb a ladder one rung at a time, we are going to build toward your biggest fear by tackling situations that cause less fear first.

For example, Katie chose performing a vocal solo as her worst fear; she rated this situation a 10 in terms of her fear and anxiety. Together, she and Jane built a fear hierarchy that incorporated this fear at the highest rung. Ideally, your hierarchy will incorporate situations ranging from about a 4 up to a 10 on the distress scale.

Some of the items on Katie's hierarchy were things that she endured while not being fully present, while others she completely avoided, such as recital solos and auditions. Notice that the fear hierarchy is ordered from the least anxiety-provoking situation to the most and that the levels of distress are evenly spaced.

Take a moment and record the feared situation that you noted above in the top rung of your fear hierarchy. Then try thinking of the first step toward that situation you could take. For example, if the situation was "going to the mall," the first step on the hierarchy might be "going to a convenience store." If going to a convenience store even seems too difficult, you might start somewhere less anxiety-inducing such as sitting in your car in the parking lot of one of the places that gives you anxiety for five minutes. Then fill in the middle steps with items that seem to naturally fit between the least distressing and most distressing items. Later on in this section, I will provide sample fear hierarchies for each type of anxiety disorder.

Now, rank the items on your hierarchy in terms of level of distress, where 0 = no distress or anxiety and 10 = the most distress or worst anxiety you've ever felt.

ACTIVITY	STRESS LEVEL (1-10)

Ideally, identify about 10 situations for your hierarchy. Items on the list can be very specific, such as telling a joke to a friend, or more general, such as talking to someone in authority. You might find it easier to list items on a separate sheet of paper or journal and then transfer them to your fear hierarchy based on the distress rating. Alternatively, you could work on your list in a program such as Microsoft Word or Excel so that you can easily rearrange feared items.

As you assembled your hierarchy, did it become clear what types of situations you find harder or easier? For example, Katie noticed that solo vocals and auditions were much more anxiety-inducing than group performances. You might notice other nuances, such as feeling more anxious when on your own versus being with a trusted friend, or feeling more fear in group settings versus talking to people one-on-one. Write any thoughts on this below.

_____

_____

_____

_____

_____

_____

_____

_____

_____

"You gain strength, courage, and confidence by every experience in which you really stop to look fear in the face. You are able to say to yourself, 'I have lived through this horror. I can take the next thing that comes along.' You must do the thing you think you cannot do." —Eleanor Roosevelt

WHY EXPOSURE WORKS

The process through which fear is reduced is called "habituation." As you become accustomed to something, your anxiety eventually levels off and decreases. If plotted on a graph, you would notice a sharp rise at the beginning and then a gradual decline—similar to a roller coaster ride. Just like that initial drop at the top of the roller coaster, when you first enter an anxiety-provoking situation, you will feel a quick rise in anxiety. However, it will eventually decrease the longer you stay in the situation. The next time you face the same situation, your anxiety level will not rise as high as it did the first time, just as the roller coaster doesn't seem quite as frightening the second time around.

Exposure therapy also works through other processes. For example, "extinction" occurs when associations you perceive between feared situations and bad outcomes are weakened. Through exposure, you also develop self-efficacy, or the belief that you can confront your fears and manage anxiety. Finally, the combination of facing fears and examining your thoughts and beliefs can result in deep emotional processing.

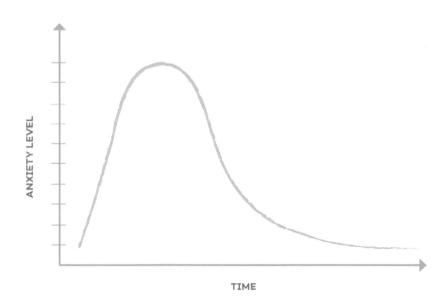

Think about a situation that caused you extreme anxiety at first but that over time you no longer feared. Can you see how just like the roller coaster ride, your fear declined the more times you faced it? Record your thoughts below.

_____

_____

_____

_____

_____

_____

_____

_____

Reminding yourself of your values can keep you moving toward a goal despite feeling fear and anxiety. In this way, fear hierarchies work best when they include situations that relate to your goals and values. For example, if you fear speaking to potential romantic partners, you might find strength to push through this fear because of wanting to find your soul mate.

Facing Your Fears

While you've worked on identifying your thoughts in situations after they happened using the Worry Diary, you now can identify them as you face a real-life situation. By facing what you fear, you will become even better at identifying and questioning negative thoughts and beliefs.

Let's consider the lowest item on Katie's fear hierarchy—performing piano accompaniment during a one-on-one lesson. This situation caused her some discomfort but not such overwhelming anxiety that she could not face it. She also chose this item because it was relevant to her day-to-day life. As a music instructor, she sometimes accompanied her students by playing the piano. However, she had found herself avoiding it more often or using recorded tapes instead of playing live.

Jane suggested that Katie make a point of playing the piano in one of her lessons the following week. Prior to entering the situation in real life, Jane suggested they talk about cognitive techniques Katie could use while in the situation to help her cope.

"Katie, I'd like you to imagine the situation. Can you think of any automatic thoughts that you might have and how you might feel?" Jane began.

"Hmm . . . well, if the student was watching me, I might be thinking that I hope I don't screw up or embarrass myself." Katie scrunched up her forehead as she thought of the situation.

"Good," Jane said. "Now, can you identify any thinking errors with what you just said? Can you think of the best and worst possible outcomes versus what is most likely to happen?"

Katie thought for a moment. "Well, the worst would be that I was shaking so much I could not play. The best would be that I wasn't anxious at all. Realistically, I would probably feel a bit anxious but get through it."

"Okay. So how does that match up with the thought that you are going to screw up or embarrass yourself?"

"I guess it doesn't really," Katie replied. "That's more of a worst-case scenario I always worry will happen."

Jane continued, "Now, let's imagine that the worst does happen and you can't play. What would you do? Would it be the end of the world?"

Katie laughed. "Well, I would feel embarrassed if the student noticed. But I would probably just pull out a tape recording to use instead."

Jane then had Katie write down two phrases to keep in her sight while she played the piano: "Nobody's perfect," and "You'll make it through." Jane instructed Katie to keep these thoughts in her mind if she started thinking negatively.

The next day, Katie sat down at the piano to accompany a student. Her hands felt a bit shaky as she started to play and she looked up to see the student frowning. Her mind quickly jumped to the thought, "She can see how anxious I am." As she glanced at the notes she had affixed to the piano, she said to herself, "Nobody's perfect. You'll make it through." She noticed that the longer she played, the less anxious she eventually felt.

Now I'd like you to conduct an exposure in your own life. Choose the lowest item on your hierarchy. Come up with a realistic and objective goal for the situation even if you feel anxious. The longer you stay in a situation the better—ideally at least 5 to 10 minutes so that by the time you finish you feel your anxiety start to level off and decrease.

Can you identify thoughts you might have while in the situation? What realistic alternatives might be helpful? Record your thoughts below.

_____

_____

_____

_____

_____

_____

_____

_____

_____

Are there any safety behaviors you would normally do in a situation like this to feel less anxious, such as leaning on a wall, covering your mouth, or bringing along a trusted friend? It's important to be aware of these behaviors and try to minimize them as you enter the situation, so that you fully face your fear.

_____

_____

_____

_____

_____

_____

_____

After engaging in the exposure, consider how it went. Did you meet the goal you set? Did you use any safety behaviors? Write your thoughts below.

_____

_____

_____

_____

_____

_____

_____

_____

_____

Did you have any unexpected thoughts that you will need to learn to better cope with in the future? Which thought was most distressing for you as you entered the exposure? Did it prove to be true or false? Has your belief changed in any way? Record your thoughts below.

_____

_____

_____

_____

_____

_____

_____

_____

_____

_____

SUCCESS AND FAILURE

Thinking in terms of success and failure is a common trap when you feel anxious. For Katie, simply playing the piano during a lesson was success—regardless of how much anxiety she felt. The goal of these exposures is to participate and feel whatever emotions arise. Don't be concerned with how well you face a situation, but rather with meeting the objective goal that you set.

Never engage in exposures that involve actual danger, such as approaching an unknown dog or visiting an unsafe location. Remember, your goal is to face your unhelpful fears, not those that exist to protect you from true danger.

FEELING STUCK? TRY THIS NEXT.

You may find yourself struggling as you work on exposures despite having the best intentions. For example, you might leave a situation before your anxiety has a chance to subside. If this happens, consider whether you chose a situation that was too overwhelming and choose something lower on your hierarchy.

A second obstacle involves feeling the same level of anxiety each time you enter a situation, no matter how many times you face it. An analogy would be a person who repeatedly rides a roller coaster and feels as much fear the tenth time as the first time. If this happens, consider whether you are fully immersing yourself in the situation or using safety behaviors. If you're giving speeches while "zoning out" to manage your anxiety, that anxiety will always loom over you as a catastrophe waiting to happen. On the other hand, if you let yourself feel your emotions in the situation, they will eventually subside and it will get easier.

Another important point is that you generally must face situations repeatedly for habituation to occur. If you speak in public only once a year, your fear never has a chance to diminish. If that's the problem, try speaking in public as often as you can—give toasts at family gatherings, tell stories to your group of friends—any event can become a public speaking encounter.

Examples of Fear Hierarchies

When constructing your own fear hierarchy, it can be helpful to see examples of how this technique is applied for different types of anxiety. To this end, I've included sample hierarchies for each of the main forms of anxiety below.

SPECIFIC PHOBIA

Specific phobias tend to be the most responsive to exposure therapy. In some cases, specific phobias can even be relieved with a single session. Whether you live with a fear of the dentist or phobia of heights, going into the feared situation and staying there until your fear is lessened is key. Below is a sample hierarchy for someone with a fear of snakes.

ACTIVITY	STRESS LEVEL (1–10)
Hold a snake in your hand	8
Have a snake placed in your lap	7
Let a snake slither over your shoe	6
Sit with a snake on a table in front of you	5
Hold a box with a snake in it	5
Look at a real snake in a closed box	5
Look at a photo of a snake	4
Think about a snake	4

SOCIAL ANXIETY DISORDER

If you have social anxiety disorder, you tend to focus on negative feedback from other people or interpret ambiguous situations as negative. For this reason, it's important to focus on realistic interpretations as you face feared situations. Does the store clerk actually dislike you or is she just tired? Will your supervisor really be that bothered if you ask for a raise? Try to challenge what you think might happen by going ahead with what you fear anyway.

ACTIVITY	STRESS LEVEL (1-10)
Give a presentation to a small group at work	8
Ask your supervisor for a raise	7
Speak to a small group of friends	6
Talk one-on-one with an acquaintance	5
Return an item to a store	5
Call a store to ask for their hours	5
Ask a stranger for the time	4
Make eye contact with a store clerk	4

PANIC DISORDER AND AGORAPHOBIA

In the case of panic disorder, interoceptive exposures will often be used. During this approach you will face the bodily sensations that you fear such as shortness of breath or a racing heart. However, you may also fear going certain places when you have panic disorder and particularly with agoraphobia.

ACTIVITY	STRESS LEVEL (1–10)
Go inside the store and buy a shopping cart full of items	7
Go inside the store and buy a few items	7
Go inside the store and buy one item	6
Park and go inside the store for a few minutes	5
Drive to the parking lot and sit parked for a few minutes	4
Drive through the parking lot and go home	4
Drive past the store	4

GENERALIZED ANXIETY DISORDER

Generalized anxiety disorder does not naturally lend itself to exposure therapy in the same way as social anxiety or specific phobias. However, you can focus on the behaviors that you have avoided because of unrealistic worry. Below is a sample hierarchy created in this manner.

ACTIVITY	STRESS LEVEL (1-10)
Take a spur-of-the-moment trip	8
Go to a restaurant that you know nothing about	6
Complete your work within scheduled hours and don't allow yourself to stay late	5
Hand in an assignment after only one round of checking your work	5
Check in with family members only once per day	4
Arrive a few minutes late to an appointment	5

One way to face your fears in generalized anxiety disorder is to imagine the worst happening. Repeatedly visualize the outcome that you fear most and accept those feelings. Eventually, you might find that you grow bored with thoughts of this catastrophic outcome and it elicits less fear and anxiety.

Review and Reflect

We've spent this chapter discussing exposure therapy and how it can make a difference in your level of anxiety. This part of the program—facing your fears—may feel frightening at first, but that's a good thing! That means you're confronting situations that you've probably avoided for a long time. Don't worry, the discomfort won't last forever, and when it goes, your level of anxiety will decrease with it.

You've now got a complete tool kit to help you begin facing your fears in real-life situations. If you prefer to blend relaxation with exposure, move on to the next chapter before completing the activity plan for this week.

At this point, take a moment to reflect on what we've discussed in this chapter. Do you have any misgivings or concerns about facing your fears directly? Write them below.

_____

_____

_____

_____

_____

_____

_____

_____

_____

_____

_____

_____

ACTIVITY PLAN

1. Complete the Worry Diary and Challenging Your Thoughts forms as before (pages 50 and 81).

2. Consult your to-do list daily.

3. Practice deep breathing five minutes each day.

4. Schedule a worry period each day.

5. Face an item on a low rung of your fear hierarchy. When that item no longer elicits strong anxiety, move up to the next item.

6. Complete the Tracking Your Progress chart at the back of the book (page 187).

7. Schedule a time to return for week 6.

How to Practice Relaxation and Mindfulness

At this point in the program, you've had a chance to examine your thoughts and beliefs and test them out in real-world situations. We've also discussed things that can hold you back, like procrastination and worry. I would be remiss to end our time together without discussing a very important part of overcoming anxiety—learning how to engage in deep relaxation and be mindful. We will examine these topics this week.

Last week, you chose a real-life challenge to face on your own. Take a moment now and reflect on how that homework assignment went. What kind of thoughts did you have while in the feared situation? Were you able to think of more realistic alternatives and stay in the situation until your level of distress went down? Record your thoughts below.

_____

_____

_____

_____

_____

_____

_____

_____

_____

_____

_____

_____

_____

_____

_____

Always on Edge: Kevin's Story

"I thought by this point in my life things would be more settled," Kevin told a friend after work. "I never thought at 52 I would be living in an apartment and only be seeing my kids on weekends."

Kevin had been divorced for two years and felt like the weight of the world was on his shoulders. The feeling of tension began the moment he woke up and did not abate until he eventually transitioned into a fitful night of sleep.

The owner of a small publishing company, Kevin attributed his restlessness to the demands of his work. "The long days and deadlines have taken a toll on me," he thought. He also attributed his fatigue to coping with life apart from his family. It was still difficult to think that his life plan had been altered.

His worries seemed worse at night, as though his brain would not shut off. He rehearsed worst-case scenarios, imagining that his business would go bankrupt and he would become homeless.

Kevin had grown up in a family in which he was told to "grin and bear it." Everyone struggles, he told himself, I am no different. I just need to find a way to release all this nervous energy that's built up. He tried working out at the gym and going out with friends for drinks, but still felt on edge all the time.

While sorting through junk mail and newspapers one day, a small ad caught his eye. "Do your worries keep you up at night? Do you have trouble relaxing? Would you like help to learn how to relax?" Kevin recognized himself in the description in the ad and felt a brief sense of hope. Before he could talk himself out of it, he sent off an email to request more information. He soon heard back that a research study was beginning at a nearby university to test the effects of relaxation training.

A few days later, he sat with one of the researchers and answered questions about how he had been feeling. At the end of the interview, he was offered the chance to participate in the study. Kevin felt nervous to start something new, but also excited that there might be light at the end of the tunnel.

A 2008 meta-analysis of 27 studies published in BMC Psychiatry showed that relaxation training had a medium- to large-size effect in the treatment of various anxiety disorders. This suggests that relaxation training is an effective way to cope with anxiety.

The Relaxation Response

Kevin sat quietly with his eyes closed. Slowly, he began to relax his muscles, starting with his feet and moving up to his face. As he relaxed, he focused on breathing deeply through his nose. Every time he exhaled, he said "calm" to himself. He continued to breathe like this for a few minutes as he lay in bed before work. Then he opened his eyes.

Sometimes, when he did this exercise in the morning, he noticed thoughts and worries taking over. When that happened, he remembered what he had been told in his meeting with the psychologist. "Try not to dwell on them and return to your breath," she had said. He did this every morning before breakfast and noticed that it was becoming easier to feel relaxed.

The roots of relaxation training began in 1975 with the book *The Relaxation Response*, written by physician Herbert Benson, founder of Harvard University's Mind/Body Medical Institute. Although it may seem that anxiety and panic are outside of your control, it is possible to encourage your body to send signals that slow down your muscles and organs and increase blood flow to your brain. This response engages the parasympathetic nervous system and is the opposite of the "fight or flight" reaction that happens during a panic attack. While there are many different approaches for attaining deep relaxation, it is quite different from sitting on a couch and watching television after work. It's not about escapism as those things are but about mindfulness, something we will cover in this week's section.

Think about your own situation. What kinds of things do you do now to relax? How well do they work for you? Perhaps you do yoga or listen to relaxation tapes. Do you make time in your busy day for relaxation? Record your thoughts in the space below.

_____

_____

_____

_____

_____

_____

_____

WHY PRACTICE RELAXATION?

As Kevin became more adept at practicing deep relaxation, he noticed his over-all well-being seemed to improve. He was sleeping better at night, had more energy during the day, and seemed to have left behind the fogginess that had clouded his thinking for so long.

Long-term anxiety and chronic stress put a strain on your body that takes a toll over time. Relaxation is a way to mitigate this effect of anxiety on your body—by reversing the tension that you experience. High levels of stress hormones can worsen stress-related conditions such as migraines, headaches, and ulcers—all of which can be helped through relaxation, according to the National Center for Complementary and Integrative Health.

Deep relaxation can lead to changes such as a decreased heart rate, lowered respiration rate, lowered blood pressure, and less muscle tension. Relaxation training is particularly helpful to reduce generalized anxiety and the frequency and severity of panic attacks. It can help you rebound from stress and experience increased energy, better sleep, and improved concentration and memory. You may even notice a boost in self-esteem and problem-solving ability. In this way, relaxation is an important add-on to what we have discussed in earlier chapters.

When you think about the impact of chronic anxiety on your overall health and well-being, can you identify any symptoms that you are having? Do you suffer from muscle tension, headaches, or gastrointestinal problems? Can you think of any positive effects that attaining deep relaxation might have for your life? Write your thoughts in the space below.

Entering Deep Relaxation

Deep relaxation can be attained through a variety of specific practices, most of which involve breath work, muscle relaxation, or visualization. Meditation is sometimes considered a state of deep relaxation, though it also overlaps with mindfulness, which we will discuss in the second half of this chapter.

BREATH WORK

Kevin breathed in deeply through his nose while slowly counting to five. Once his lungs were full, he paused for another count of five. Then he slowly exhaled through his mouth until all his breath was fully exhaled. He then breathed in and out normally for two breaths, before repeating the same counting technique. He continued this breathing exercise for about five minutes. Every time he exhaled he repeated the word "calm" silently to himself and felt his whole body let go.

We discussed abdominal breathing in a previous chapter. This type of breathing involves inhaling deeply from the diaphragm instead of from the chest. Breathing from the chest can worsen panic and anxiety and lead to hyperventilation in the case of panic disorder. In contrast, deep abdominal breathing encourages the body to relax as you take in more oxygen.

The Calming Breath Exercise is adapted from yoga and can be used to quickly enter a state of deep relaxation. To practice this type of breathing, follow these steps:

1. Breathe in through your nose and deeply into your abdomen while slowly counting to five.

2. Pause for a count of five.

3. Exhale slowly through your mouth to the count of five. Say a phrase to yourself as you do, such as "peace," "relax," or "calm."

4. Breathe in and out normally for two breaths.

5. Repeat steps 1 to 4 a total of 10 times, or for about 5 to 10 minutes.

Take a moment now and pay attention to your own breath. Are you breathing shallowly from your chest or deeply from your abdomen? Do you take quick breaths or slow breaths? Place a hand on your stomach and notice whether it rises and falls as you breathe. Make notes below about what you notice about your breathing.

_____

_____

_____

_____

_____

_____

MUSCLE RELAXATION

As part of relaxation training, Kevin was instructed to tense and relax different muscles throughout his body. Each Wednesday, he met with a therapist who read through a script directing him to focus on each part of his body in order.

Eventually, he looked forward to Wednesdays because of how good it made him feel. The feeling of relaxation generated in these sessions extended into his daily life. He continued practicing at home and was relieved to have found a way to ease his tension and eliminate his insomnia.

PROGRESSIVE MUSCLE RELAXATION

Muscle relaxation is a key method for entering a state of deep relaxation. Progressive muscle relaxation (PMR) is a systematic technique that was developed by American physician Edmund Jacobsen in the 1920s. PMR is particularly helpful if your anxiety is associated with feeling tense or uptight, having headaches or feeling tightness, or having insomnia and racing thoughts.

If you wish to practice PMR, follow the steps below. Also, see the Resources section at the back of this book for information on audio files that can be used to enhance your practice of this technique.

Plan to practice for 20 to 30 minutes at the same time each day, such as when you first wake up, when going to bed, or before a meal—digestion can interfere with deep relaxation.

1. Choose a quiet location free from distractions.

2. Lie down on a bed or couch or sit in a recliner so that your body is completely supported. If you tend to fall asleep when relaxed, you may prefer sitting to lying down.

3. Loosen tight clothing; take off your shoes, jewelry, and so on.

4. Adopt a detached attitude free of any worry about how you are doing. Make taking care of yourself a priority. Don't *try* to relax, just let yourself go.

5. Take three deep abdominal breaths and exhale slowly as you imagine tension flowing out of your body.

6. Tense and then relax the following muscle groups in your body. Tense for 10 seconds and then abruptly release. Then, relax for 15 to 20 seconds and notice the sudden feeling of limpness and how the muscle feels relaxed compared to tensed. Make sure other muscles are relaxed while you focus on one group. If you have pain or strain in any area, omit it from practice.

- Hands: clench your fists
- Biceps: draw forearm toward your shoulder
- Triceps: extend arm and lock elbow
- Forehead: raise eyebrows
- Eyes: tightly shut eyelids

- Jaw: open mouth widely
- Neck: extend head backward
- Shoulders: raise toward your ears
- Back: push your shoulder blades toward each other
- Chest: hold a deep breath
- Stomach: suck it in
- Lower back: arch it up
- Buttocks: squeeze together
- Thighs: squeeze your muscles
- Calves: pull toes toward you
- Feet: curl toes downward

7. As you practice, focus on your muscles. Don't let your mind wander.

8. Scan your body for any remaining tension. Repeat the above steps for any area that still feels tense.

After you finish, imagine a wave of relaxation spreading through your body, starting at your head and flowing down to your toes.

An alternative method for muscle relaxation involves imagining each part of your body relaxing, starting with your feet and moving slowly through your body up to your head. Some people prefer this type of relaxation because it does not involve the effort of tensing muscles.

Take some time now to try out some of the exercises described above. Tense your fist tightly for 10 seconds and then abruptly release it for 15 to 20 seconds. Do you notice a difference between the tensed and relaxed muscles? Schedule a time and place that you will practice muscle relaxation and make a note of it below.

_____

_____

_____

_____

_____

VISUALIZATION AND GUIDED IMAGERY

Kevin imagines himself lying in a hammock at a friend's cottage. He hears the waves rolling onto shore, helping him relax. It's a nice warm day and the sun is just starting to set out over the lake. Waves gently lap at the shore as boats come and go. He can smell someone barbecuing in the distance as the breeze passes through. He feels very calm and relaxed in this favorite spot.

ENGAGING THE SENSES

Visualization is the perfect partner for PMR. Imagining yourself in a peaceful scene, be it the beach, your backyard, or wherever you find relaxing, will help you become absorbed in the moment. When done right, visualization can be a form of self-hypnosis.

Now I'd like you to take a moment and describe your own peaceful scene. Be sure to use words that reflect what you see, hear, touch, and smell—this will help you feel like you are in the situation and encourage a state of deep relaxation. Describe the colors you see, the time of day, whether it's warm or cold, and who else is there. Write down your description in the space below.

_____

_____

_____

_____

_____

_____

_____

_____

_____

Take some time now to imagine yourself in your peaceful scene, and feel a sense of peace flow through your body. Allow these feelings to grow stronger. Revisit this scene after each deep relaxation practice. This will help build the habit and allow you to return to this favorite scene when you need to calm down.

Alternately, you may prefer to use a guided visualization, during which you simply listen to a CD or MP3, such as those suggested in the Resources section. If you choose this route, plan to listen at the same time every day.

_____

_____

_____

_____

_____

_____

_____

_____

_____

_____

_____

_____

_____

_____

_____

OTHER RELAXATION STRATEGIES

In addition to deep breathing, muscle relaxation, and visualization, you may find some of the relaxation techniques listed below to be helpful.

Self-hypnosis: This technique can be used to enter deep relaxation and combat tension. Hypnosis involves entering a trance or deep state of focused relaxation, and then having your subconscious mind accept suggestions.

Autogenic training: This technique is similar to meditation, during which you repeat a series of statements to yourself about different parts of your body. This works to influence the functioning of your autonomic nervous system, including your heart rate.

Biofeedback: Biofeedback involves the use of tools to measure your body's physiological responses to stress, so that you can learn to control them. Generally, this involves measuring heart rate, muscle tension, or even brain waves. However, you can practice a simpler form of biofeedback at home by paying attention to when your body seems tense or you are breathing shallowly.

Yoga: Yoga postures promote relaxation in the same way as progressive muscle relaxation. Yoga can help you release tension, improve concentration, and relax.

Music: Listen to relaxing music while doing other tasks or as a primary activity. Be sure to choose music that has a relaxing and calming tone rather than that which will evoke strong emotions. Check the Resources section for suggestions of calming music.

Meditation: We will discuss meditation more in the next section on mindfulness. For now, understand that meditation is a method to help you feel balanced, calm, and focused.

What If I Can't Slow Down?

When Kevin first joined the study, he found it hard to practice relaxation exercises at home. "I have so much to do, how can I just lie there for 30 minutes?" His therapist pointed to Kevin's hands, which he had been drumming nervously on the top of the therapist's desk. "Kevin, perhaps the fact you can't slow down and take 30 minutes to relax is a sign that it is something you really need?"

Often we start out enthusiastic when we begin something new. I tend to do the same when attempting a new eating plan or exercise routine. I spend a week diligently following the plan and meeting the goals I've set for myself. Then routine steps in and pulls me back to my old patterns. Slowly, I abandon the new habits I was trying to foster. If only I'd stuck with it for a month, it might have gotten easier—we know it takes about 30 days for a new habit to become ingrained.

Take a moment and consider the obstacles that might interfere with you engaging in deep relaxation daily. Is it lack of time or location? Do you feel as though sitting and relaxing is frivolous? Think about potential stumbling blocks and write them in the space below.

_____

_____

_____

_____

_____

Now, look back over what you have written. Can you think of solutions to these problems? If time is an issue, consider whether making relaxation a priority would free up time in other areas of your life. How much time do you spend worrying about or avoiding situations? Think about this time as an investment in yourself that will pay off in the long run.

If a suitable location is a problem, could you do it in bed first thing in the morning or last thing at night? Remember that you are working on a radical shift in your attitude and lifestyle. Part of that commitment involves making time and making relaxation a priority. Write down your thoughts below.

_____

_____

_____

_____

_____

For some people, entering a state of deep relaxation can provoke feelings of anxiety, as emotions are uncovered. If practicing relaxation exercises seems to make you more anxious, try practicing for shorter periods in the beginning and eventually extending them.

Mindfulness

Kevin had a habit of getting caught up in the whirlwind of his thoughts and worries. While he was getting better at managing tension in his body and sleeping better at night, there was still a piece of the puzzle that was missing. He learned that in the coming weeks of the study he would be taught how to practice a technique known as "mindfulness," so he could let those worried thoughts float past him instead of getting stuck on them.

Struggling against anxiety tends to invite more anxiety into your life. However, if you can accept that anxiety will exist in your life, but you remain open and aware, you may find your anxiety diminishes. This concept is known as mindfulness and is rooted in the principles of Buddhism.

Jon Kabat-Zinn, PhD, author of the book *Wherever You Go, There You Are*, developed a treatment for anxiety rooted in this concept: mindfulness-based stress reduction (MBSR). The basis for this technique is that detachment from anxious thoughts and feelings allows you to view them as transient. This makes you less likely to react and make a problem worse than it is. When we identify ourselves with our thoughts, it's hard to separate from them. Yet when we see our thoughts as entities separate from ourselves, we can observe them and let them go.

Can you think of a time in your life when you made something worse than it was because you became stuck on a thought or worry? Write down any observations in the space below.

_____

_____

_____

_____

_____

_____

"You can't stop the waves, but you can learn to surf." —Jon Kabat-Zinn

How to Be Mindful

Being mindful seems inherently simple. In practice, however, being observant takes time to develop as a skill. It's best to start being mindful for short periods of time, such as taking one minute several times a day to breathe deeply and notice what is happening around you. Be curious and present in the moment in which you find yourself.

MEDITATION

When you think of meditation, do you picture a room full of people sitting cross-legged, chanting "om?" While this might not be far from the truth, meditation forms a part of many other practices that you might not immediately think of such as yoga, visualization, and mindfulness. Meditation is simply the practice of learning how to pay attention.

Most of us spend our days busy with the external world. If your mind is always busy and racing, it helps to slow it down and witness the world around you without judgment. When you reach this state of awareness, it will be easier to stand on the outside of your fear and anxiety as a witness rather than becoming stuck in your stream of thoughts. In this way, meditation helps break up obsessional thought patterns and reduce chronic anxiety and worry.

Meditation can involve focusing on something specific, such as an object, word, or your breath. It can also be non-concentrative, as in the practice of mindfulness.

BODY SCAN

As you meditate, it can be helpful to do a body scan. This involves bringing attention to each part of your body. Allow your feelings to come to the surface and release them. You can complete this exercise lying down or sitting in a recliner. Focus on your breathing first. Then notice your toes. Breathe through your body and expel tension out through your toes. Focus on sensations, tension, and feelings in each part of your body and then breathe them out through that part of your body.

Conducting a body scan helps you identify areas in which you are holding tension and learn to release it. Do this as often as you feel necessary or when tension arises.

Below is a brief meditation exercise that you can try:

1. Sit upright with your feet flat on the floor.

2. Pay attention to your breath. Observe it, but don't try to change it.

3. If you feel the urge to focus on something else, resist it.

4. If you find yourself thinking of expectations and anxious thoughts, gently bring your attention back to your breath. Say to yourself, "That is just a thought."

5. Sit quietly like this for 10 minutes.

6. Open your eyes and notice how you feel without judging your performance.

As you practiced this basic meditation, what did you notice? Did you find yourself distracted by things in the external environment? Did anxious thoughts pass through your mind? Record your thoughts below.

_____

_____

_____

_____

_____

_____

_____

_____

If you find it hard to sit long enough to practice meditation or relaxation, try engaging in physical exercise to burn off excess energy and make it easier to let go.

Shifting Awareness

Mindfulness involves the act of shifting awareness. This allows you to notice and accept your feelings but witness them as an observer. It also allows you to look at your thoughts more objectively, decide which require action, and which might be better to let go. Below are examples of how you might shift awareness for each type of anxiety.

Panic disorder: In the case of panic disorder, you might move from a narrow focus on bodily sensations and feelings of fear toward a broad awareness of your feelings and thoughts. "I can't breathe" might be replaced with "I am having the thought that I can't breathe." You might then conclude that the shortness of breath you are feeling is a passing feeling of discomfort that you can ignore.

Agoraphobia: For those with agoraphobia, you might move from "I can't leave the house alone" to "I am worrying about leaving the house alone." The first statement sounds like a fact, while the second observes that it is just a transient state, allowing you to make decisions more objectively.

Social anxiety disorder: If you have social anxiety disorder, you might shift from thoughts such as "Everyone is judging me" to "I am having the thought that everyone is judging me." Letting go of this thought could be the natural next step.

Generalized anxiety disorder: In generalized anxiety disorder, there might be a shift from "What if I lose my job?" to "I am worrying what would happen if I lose my job." If it seems objectively that the odds of losing your job are small, you can confidently let this thought go.

Specific phobia: In specific phobia, you might move from "Dogs are dangerous" to "I am having the thought that dogs are dangerous." If you encounter a dog that is known to be friendly, you would then be able to let go of that thought.

Think about your own situation. What would it mean for you to be able to shift your awareness to being an observer of your own thoughts instead of

caught up in them? Choose some of the thoughts and beliefs that you identified in earlier chapters. Can you identify that they are transient states rather
than absolute facts? Record your thoughts below.

_____

_____

_____

_____

_____

_____

_____

_____

_____

"What you resist, persists." —Carl Jung

PASSENGERS ON THE BUS

As with mindfulness, acceptance and commitment therapy (ACT), which we
discussed briefly during week two, draws heavily on the values of Buddhist
philosophy and acceptance of negative thoughts. ACT involves principles of
cognitive defusion (detachment from thoughts), acceptance, being mindful in
the present moment, being observant, honoring your values, and committing
to action that is in line with your values.

ACT involves the use of metaphors to explain ideas. Below is one metaphor that might be helpful as we close out this chapter.

Imagine that a bus represents your mind and the passengers on the bus symbolize different internal experiences that you have. You are the driver and you exist separately from the passengers on the bus. You can listen and hear what the passengers say, but you do not have to believe it to be true or adhere to their demands.

These passengers cannot touch the mechanics of the bus. You are the driver and you control the direction and speed of the bus. You can stop the bus and ask rude passengers to leave, but this would take time away from moving forward. Instead, you as the driver can acknowledge their presence on the bus while you remain in control.

As in this metaphor, internal experiences will always arise, but you are in ultimate control of the way you behave. Are you in control of the choices you make in your life or have you let passengers (your anxious thoughts) take the wheel? Are your choices aligned with your values, or are you letting the passengers derail you? Do you believe what the passengers on the bus are telling you? Write your thoughts below.

_____

_____

_____

_____

_____

_____

_____

_____

_____

Review and Reflect

Congratulations on your work up until this point. Developing new habits requires patience—and maintaining them in the long term involves dedication. During the next week, we'll integrate everything that we've learned so far and generate some ideas to prevent you from slipping back into old habits.

_____

_____

_____

_____

_____

_____

_____

_____

_____

_____

_____

_____

_____

_____

ACTIVITY PLAN

1. Complete the Worry Diary and Challenging Your Thoughts forms as needed (pages 50 and 81).

2. Keep working on your to-do list.

3. Keep your scheduled worry period for dealing with worries.

4. Face an item on a low rung of your fear hierarchy. When that item no longer elicits strong anxiety, move up to the next item.

5. Choose one or more relaxation techniques to practice at a regular time each day.

6. Engage in one minute of mindful awareness a few times each day.

7. Complete the Tracking Your Progress chart at the back of the book (page 187).

8. Schedule a time to return for week 7.

Coming Full Circle

When you think of "coming full circle," you probably imagine ending up at the point at which you began. While my hope is that you've done more of a 180-degree turn in terms of your anxiety, I hope that this relief of your anxiety has also helped you return to your true self, in whatever way is meaningful for you. That will be the focus of this final chapter: to integrate what you've learned in a way that helps you reach your goals and live the life you've always wanted.

Last week, we discussed the importance of incorporating relaxation and mindfulness into your plan for overcoming anxiety. I asked you to practice a relaxation exercise daily and to include a few one-minute mindfulness periods into each day. Now take a moment to reflect on how well you were able to integrate relaxation and mindfulness during your daily routine. Note any obstacles you faced, such as finding the time or being able to wind down. Record your thoughts below.

_____

_____

_____

_____

A Self-Help Journey

Kendra looked back on the goals she had set for herself less than two months ago. "I can't believe how I felt at the time. So much has changed."

At the time, she had been struggling daily. Between work and a busy social life, she had goals she wanted to achieve but anxiety was holding her back. On the outside, she appeared to be in control, an image she was careful to project. Always the first to arrive at work, dressed neatly, and relentlessly deadline-conscious, she was known for her willingness to help others when asked.

What most people did not know, and what she would never share, was that underneath her perfect exterior she felt like a mess. Her stomach was in knots. She awoke every night at 3 a.m. and could not fall back to sleep, because her mind was racing. Sometimes her anxiety slipped out when she was with other people, such as through nervous chatter or habits. Her schedule had also become overloaded to the point of breaking, and she had started letting people down because of it.

As anxiety invaded her life more and more, she found herself coping with feelings of sadness. Her nightly glass of red wine had turned into two, and then three. One night, after a few glasses of wine, she was browsing on Amazon and came across self-help books for anxiety. "Why not?" she thought and ordered one.

In the weeks that ensued, she followed along chapter-by-chapter, implementing the homework activities. She learned about how her anxious thoughts fueled her feelings of anxiety, how to deal with uncertainty and perfectionism, and how to use relaxation strategies. As she got closer to the end of the book, she started to feel uneasy about the future, thinking, "I'm feeling better, but what if it doesn't last? What if I end up back where I started?"

"Don't believe every worried thought you have. Worried thoughts are notoriously inaccurate." —Renee Jain, founder of GoZen.com

VITAMINS AND MINERALS FOR ANXIETY

Vitamins and minerals play a key role in good mental health; deficiencies in certain vitamins and minerals could make your anxiety worse.

Vitamin C: One small, randomized, controlled study of 42 high school students in 2015 showed that oral supplementation of vitamin C reduced anxiety levels. It's easy to get your daily dose: One large orange provides you with 100 percent of your daily need for vitamin C.

B Complex: The B complex vitamins are a family of eight B vitamins, including B_1 (thiamine) and B_9 (folic acid). A double-blind study of 80 healthy males showed that daily use of a B complex multivitamin resulted in significantly lower self-reported anxiety and stress. Foods such as whole grains, dairy products, eggs, meat, beans, seeds, nuts, and soy are good sources of B vitamins.

Zinc: One study of rats fed a zinc-deficient diet for one to two weeks showed an increase in anxiety-like behavior. Include zinc in your diet by eating foods such as beef, pork, poultry (dark meat), nuts, whole grains, and legumes.

Iron: A deficiency in iron may be implicated in anxiety. High-iron foods include beef, liver, whole grains, nuts, sunflower seeds, dark leafy greens, tofu, and dark chocolate.

Calcium: Research has also shown links between calcium levels and anxiety. Get your calcium from milk, yogurt, dark leafy greens, cheese, broccoli, green beans, and almonds.

Chromium: Like iron and calcium, a lack of chromium has also been linked to anxiety. Foods such as processed meats, whole grains, green beans, broccoli, nuts, and egg yolks are high in chromium.

While the best sources of vitamins and minerals come from eating healthy food, taking a supplement could also help you meet your daily requirements. Choose a good quality multivitamin with dosages of vitamins and minerals that match daily-recommended values. If you've got questions about supplements, be sure to talk to your doctor.

Your Progress

We discussed earlier the importance of goal setting for making progress. The second component to this is reviewing the goals that you set for yourself.

Kendra looked at the goals she had set two months ago:

Reduce my overall anxiety level.

Become better at saying "no" when overloaded with requests.

Have more downtime for myself.

Stop using alcohol to cope.

Accept not being perfect.

"I definitely feel less anxious," she thought while looking at the list. "I've also created more downtime. I haven't worked on a weekend in at least a month. I'm getting better at saying no when I don't have time but could still use some work on that. I've also replaced the extra wine with a nightly walk." She frowned as she looked at the last goal. "I'm still too hard on myself though. Perfectionism is tough to get over."

Kendra's overall anxiety had declined, but there were still some specific areas she needed to address. She had done well introducing relaxation and mindfulness into her daily routine but still struggled at times when challenging her anxious thoughts.

Determined not to slip into old ways, she made a plan to follow after she was done with the book. She also suggested a mindfulness meditation retreat to a friend. In the past, she might have thought of something like that as frivolous, but she was now ready to be fully invested in her well-being.

In week 1 of this program, you set some general goals. I'd like you to take a moment now and look back on the goals you set. Throughout the seven weeks, you also set more specific goals, such as when completing exposures. Think about how you've done in meeting the general goals you set and how the specific goals helped you reach them. Write your thoughts below about how you did.

_____

_____

_____

_____

_____

_____

As part of this process, I also asked you to keep a record of your progress using the Tracking Your Progress chart in the back of this book (page 187). Have a look at your chart and record your thoughts below. Did your anxiety decrease, remain level, or increase? Can you think of reasons for the trend that you see?

_____

_____

_____

_____

_____

_____

We've covered a lot of ground, including understanding and changing negative beliefs, facing your fears, managing panic, worry, and perfectionism, and practicing relaxation and mindfulness. Of these areas, which do you feel most confident about and where do you think you need more work? Write your thoughts below.

_____

_____

_____

_____

_____

_____

Part of what keeps us motivated to change is success, whether a small victory or big accomplishment. While you may not have reached every goal that you set seven weeks ago, you likely had some success along the way. This could be anything from petting a neighbor's dog to leaving your house for the first time in months. Take a moment, think of what you've achieved—no matter how seemingly insignificant it is—and write it below.

_____

_____

_____

_____

_____

_____

Now, considering everything that we've discussed, are there particular areas in which you feel you still need improvement? Record your thoughts below.

_____

_____

_____

_____

_____

_____

_____

_____

_____

Learning to be assertive is an important part of overcoming social anxiety disorder. Assertiveness does not mean being aggressive; rather, it refers to openly sharing your needs so that others are in a better position to respond to them.

WHAT'S HOLDING YOU BACK?

If you identified in the previous section that your progress was stalled, let's take a moment to identify why. If we know the "why" then we can begin to work on how to effectively fix it. Did a stressful life event interfere with your ability to complete this program, such as the illness of a family member or job loss? Were you coping with other issues at the same time such as depression or substance abuse, which were more deeply rooted than your anxiety? Sometimes, starting again at a less stressful time in your life or receiving help for other issues that overlap with anxiety works best. Record your thoughts below.

_____

_____

_____

_____

_____

_____

_____

_____

Not being fully invested in completing CBT exercises can also sometimes impede progress. If you did not do exposures regularly or for a long enough period, they would have had a minimal effect. If this is the case, take advantage of opportunities for exposures and don't stop them too soon. If this has been a problem for you, write down a plan for engaging in exposures.

_____

_____

_____

_____

_____

_____

_____

_____

Time for Review

Now, let's compile a list of each of the core principles that we've discussed for you to easily reference. Keep a copy of this list with you for when you are feeling anxious. As you get better at identifying and challenging your thoughts automatically in your daily life, you can stop using the Worry Diary and Challenging Your Thoughts forms. If you find that your understanding or memory of any section is poor, go back and review that section or chapter a second time.

CORE PRINCIPLES

The following is a list of key practices that we've introduced in the last several weeks. Keep working on each of these strategies for the best long-term results.

- Set goals for yourself and review them often.

- Distance yourself from your thoughts—they are your perceptions and not necessarily factual.

- Set a daily worry time to focus on worries that arise throughout the day.

- Replace unhelpful thoughts and core beliefs with more realistic alternatives.

- Reinforce helpful thoughts and beliefs through positive affirmations.

- Keep a list of evidence in support of your new core beliefs.

- Overcome avoidance by gradually facing the situations you fear.

- Keep a to-do list and review it often.

- Break down large tasks into smaller steps.

- Ask yourself how realistic your expectations are of yourself in any situation.

- Reward yourself for completing difficult tasks.

- Use organizational tools and try to delegate what you can.

- Exercise regularly, get adequate sleep, and eat a balanced diet.

- Practice at least one relaxation technique daily, such as deep breathing, muscle relaxation, or visualization.

- Avoid caffeine and other stimulants that can make anxiety worse.

- Don't fight against your anxiety—lean into it instead.

- Worrying is not problem-solving, be sure not to confuse the two.

- Keep a journal to write down your worries.

- Don't rely on safety behaviors when in situations that cause you anxiety.

When Anxiety Returns

Your journey toward living well despite anxiety does not end when you finish this book. You will need to continue to apply what you've learned about CBT, relaxation, and mindfulness in your daily life to prevent anxiety from returning. In the next section, let's consider events that may lead to a return of troublesome anxiety.

RELAPSE TRIGGERS

Kendra was feeling good about herself and her progress. She had implemented a plan to continue to practice CBT and mindfulness strategies daily. She was feeling so good, in fact, that she decided to embark on a new challenge. She enrolled in a part-time MBA program, something that had been a goal of hers for a while. However, she found that as her studies began, many of her old habits and ways of thinking returned. Despite her best work at maintaining the gains from self-help, this new stress in her life seemed to be triggering a return to an earlier state.

If you've been feeling well and then notice a return of troublesome anxiety, it can be disheartening. This may happen for several reasons, even if you are continuing to practice CBT strategies.

I remember participating in a golf tournament when I worked as a summer student on the greens staff of a local golf course. Having heard I was a good golfer, my supervisor invited me to join his team. Though I had never felt nervous before playing golf, each time I approached my tee shot that afternoon I unconsciously tensed up. Every drive dribbled about 10 feet off the tee and my confidence went with it. While I had played lots of golf before, I'd never been in a position in which someone was counting on me to play well.

Just like me, you may find yourself in a situation outside of what you've faced and notice that your anxiety goes up. Take a moment and consider new situations that could arise, such as giving a toast at a family meal or having to take a detour to work. Could you add these to your list of situations to face?

_____

_____

_____

_____

_____

_____

_____

"You may not control all the events that happen to you, but you can decide not to be reduced by them." —Maya Angelou

New life stressors such as changing jobs or experiencing a loss may also trigger old feelings of anxiety. In addition, experiencing a traumatic anxiety-related event, such as freezing up during a performance, might cause your anxiety to return. However, it's important to begin facing situations again as soon as possible so that your anxiety does not return.

PREVENTING RELAPSE

While relapse is common, it does not have to mean an end to the hard work you've done. We've all faced situations in which we fell back into old patterns or habits after a period of doing better. Recognize that anxiety is no different and that you will have better periods and times when you struggle. Just like with diet and exercise, you will need to continue to work hard from time to time to maintain the gains you've realized. Below are some strategies you can use to reduce the likelihood of a relapse.

Continue completing exposures: While it may be tempting to think that once your anxiety has subsided you can stop facing what you fear, continue doing exposures once in a while. Otherwise, your fear may return.

After a traumatic event, return to the situation as soon as possible: For example, if you have a panic attack while driving your car, return to driving as soon as you feel comfortable so that avoidance does not reignite your anxiety.

Continue to adhere to the principles of CBT: Keep identifying and challenging your thoughts long after you've finished these seven weeks. If you find yourself slipping into old thinking patterns, go back and review the relevant chapters and consult your medical professional as needed.

Practice facing your fears in a wide range of situations: As you work on exposures, try to identify as many different types of scenarios as possible, so that you don't find yourself in a situation that you've not practiced. If this does happen, add it to your list of exposures.

Engage in "overlearning": Whenever possible, do exposures to the point that they become boring, and work your way up to situations much more difficult than what you ever expect to face. If you've gone to the top of a skyscraper, that fourth floor balcony will become much easier.

Get enough rest and take care of yourself physically: Lack of sleep or poor physical health can exacerbate anxiety. Take time to take care of yourself.

Understand that you will continue to experience anxiety: Your goal in this program is not to eliminate anxiety. Rather, learn that anxiety can be managed before it grows out of control.

Understand that the goal of CBT is for you to become your own therapist: If you feel as though you're losing your lifeline at the end of this program, remember that the goal all along was for you to apply the principles on your own.

Develop a support network: Join a support group for the type of anxiety disorder that you have. Talking about your overlapping experiences will help you feel less alone.

Practice gratitude: Show gratitude for the good in your life; this will help give you perspective and keep you focused on the present.

Be kind to yourself: Nobody is perfect. Know that you can overcome a relapse and get back on track. Much like you should not give up on healthy eating after one bad meal, don't ever give up on your mental wellness after a bout of anxiety. As you look over this list, can you identify a few strategies that you think will be most helpful in the coming weeks as you continue your journey? Write them below.

_____

_____

_____

_____

_____

_____

"The best use of imagination is creativity. The worst use of imagination is anxiety."
—Deepak Chopra

Finding Help

Sometimes, despite your best efforts, the struggles that you face cannot be overcome alone. If you find that your anxiety is severe and not responsive to self-help strategies, it is important to seek help in the form of traditional treatment such as anxiety medication or therapy. I've included some online therapist directories in the Resources section at the back of the book to help you in this endeavor. You can also ask your primary care doctor for a referral to a specialist.

The Best Is Yet to Come

As we come to the close of this chapter, know that your journey does not end here. Whether you've celebrated small or large victories, you are capable of so much more. As I mentioned at the start of this chapter, I hope that learning to manage your anxiety has helped you move closer to a true version of yourself.

DROP THE ROPE

One popular acceptance and commitment therapy metaphor is referred to as "dropping the rope." Imagine you are on one side of a bottomless pit. On the other side of the pit stands a huge menacing monster, which represents your anxiety. Between you is a rope, and you engage in a tug-of-war as you attempt to pull the monster—your anxiety—into the bottomless pit so that you don't have to face it anymore. However, pull hard as you might, you cannot get the monster into the pit, and instead become agitated in the process. During ACT therapy, you learn that if instead you "drop the rope" and stop trying to fight against your anxiety, you can learn to live with it peacefully. Just as the tug-of-war drains your energy, so does fighting against your anxiety. Instead, if you can learn to accept some anxiety, you can move on with your life despite it.

Take a moment now and imagine the person you most want to be. Perhaps you would like to travel, pursue a meaningful career, have a family, develop friendships, or simply go about each day in a calm and purposeful way.

Write down this vision of the person that you would like to become on your journey toward good mental health. If you ever feel as though the journey is too difficult, return to this vision of the person you want to be. Use it as a guidepost toward your goals.

_____

_____

_____

_____

_____

_____

_____

_____

_____

_____

_____

_____

_____

_____

_____

Final Reflection

I am so pleased that you chose to embark on this journey. While I'm sure it was not always easy, I am hopeful that you've noticed changes in your life that made it worthwhile. Remember to implement the ideas that we discussed in this chapter if at any point you find yourself relapsing. One final time, I'd like you to write down how you are feeling as we end the program.

ACTIVITY PLAN

1. Continue to identify and challenge your negative thoughts and beliefs, and practice exposures.

2. Continue to include a regular worry period, relaxation period, and a bit of mindful awareness each day.

3. Keep working through and adding to your to-do list.

4. Complete the Tracking Your Progress chart at the back of the book (page 187).

Conclusion

In the Long Term

In the following pages, I've provided some additional resources for you to consult as you move forward after these 7 weeks. These include books, websites, and apps that I believe to be useful. While you may no longer be actively engaging in a program to overcome your anxiety, I encourage you to continue to reread sections of this book that you found particularly helpful.

In addition, be sure to continue applying all of the techniques that you've learned, including identifying and reformulating negative thoughts, relaxation training, and mindfulness. When it comes to maintaining your new outlook, the whole is truly bigger than the sum of its parts. Using a combination of strategies will help support your efforts in the weeks, months, and years to come.

At this time, I also invite you to do two things: Make peace with your past and focus on being in the present. Whatever impact anxiety has had on you in the past, be it stopping you from leaving the house or preventing you from pursuing a career, recognize that you don't have to continue to dwell on what has happened. While it's important to understand the role of anxiety in your life, focusing too much on what's gone wrong will make it difficult for you to welcome everything that's about to go right. Think of yourself as moving forward with a blank slate from this point. You are in charge of writing a new story about yourself, one that can be of your choosing.

If you do find yourself slipping back into old habits, I'd encourage you to ask a simple question: "Am I acting in a way that is in alignment with my life values and purpose?" Or to put it another way: Are you letting anxiety rule your life? You likely won't ever be completely free from anxiety, but I hope you will continue to practice moving your way through it so you can achieve your loftiest dreams.

Finally, if you are like me and find yourself motivated by goals, continue to review the goals you've set for yourself. Add new ones as appropriate and reward yourself for those you've achieved. Above all else, value yourself and continue to seek improvement, and the rest should fall into place.

TRACKING
YOUR PROGRESS

The following section offers a way for you to visually track your progress over the 7-week program.

INSTRUCTIONS

Rate each item on the next page on a scale from 1 to 7, where 1 = much less than at the start of this program, 4 = not different from the start, and 7 = much more than at the start. Write your ratings in the column that corresponds to the current week of the program. Then add up the ratings for each week and write the totals in the bottom row. Finally, plot your total score on the chart that follows for the corresponding week.

	WEEK 1	WEEK 2	WEEK 3	WEEK 4	WEEK 5	WEEK 6	WEEK 7
How often do you experience panic, anxiety, or worry?							
How much anxiety, worry, or panic do you feel when it happens?							
How often do you avoid situations or things because of your anxiety or worry?							
How much does your anxiety or worry interfere with your work/school or daily life?							
TOTAL SCORE							

NOTES

_____

_____

_____

_____

ANXIETY CHANGE INDEX

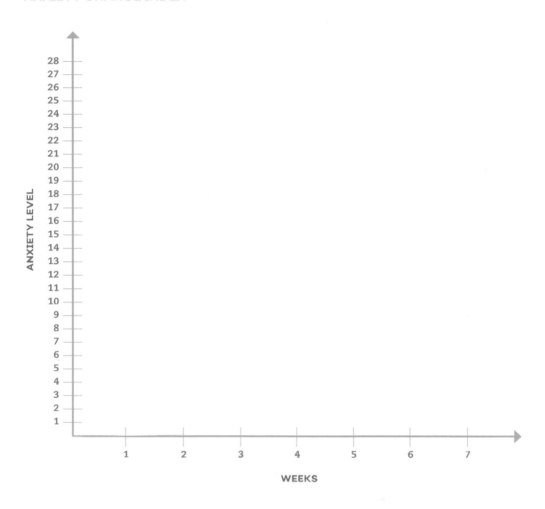

_____

_____

_____

_____

	WEEK 1	WEEK 2	WEEK 3	WEEK 4	WEEK 5	WEEK 6	WEEK 7
How often do you experience panic, anxiety, or worry?	—	4	4	3	3	3	2
How much anxiety, worry, or panic do you feel when it happens?	—	4	3	3	3	2	2
How often do you avoid situations or things because of your anxiety or worry?	—	4	4	4	3	3	3
How much does your anxiety or worry interfere with your work/school or daily life?	—	4	3	3	3	2	2
TOTAL SCORE	—	16	14	13	12	10	9

NOTES

_____

_____

_____

_____

ANXIETY CHANGE INDEX

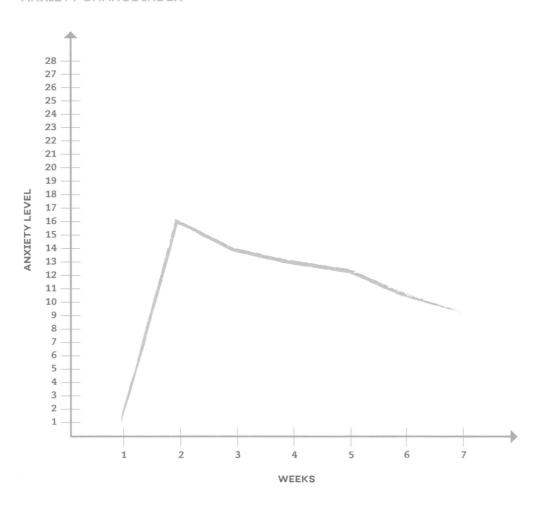

NOTES

_____

_____

_____

_____

Appendix B

BLANK FORMS

WORRY DIARY

DATE/TIME	SITUATION	ANXIETY RATING (0–10)	FEELINGS, THOUGHTS, ACTIONS

THOUGHT(S)

EVENT

EMOTION(S)

NOTES

_____

_____

_____

_____

_____

_____

_____

_____

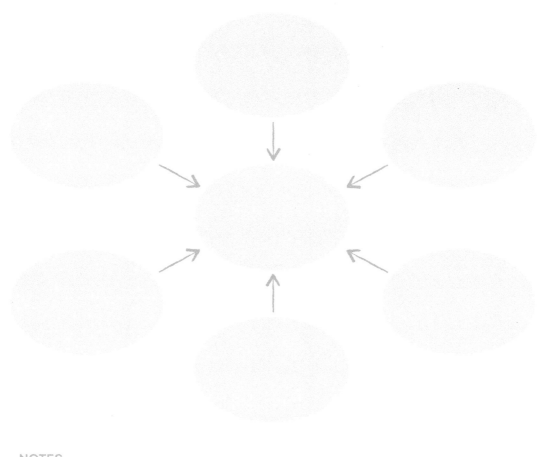

NOTES

_____

_____

_____

_____

_____

EVIDENCE FOR MY THOUGHT	EVIDENCE AGAINST MY THOUGHT

NOTES

FEAR HIERARCHY

ACTIVITY	STRESS LEVEL (1-10)

NOTES

_____

_____

_____

_____

_____

RESOURCES

Here I've included resources that will be useful to you from a self-help perspective or in conjunction with traditional treatment. I've included resources that are grounded in evidence-based treatments, as these have been shown to be effective in managing anxiety.

Books

Antony, Martin M., and Peter J. Norton. *The Anti-Anxiety Workbook: Proven Strategies to Overcome Worry, Phobias, Panic, and Obsessions.* New York: The Guilford Press, 2008.

Bourne, Edmund. *The Anxiety and Phobia Workbook.* Oakland, CA: New Harbinger Publications, 2015.

Boyes, Alice. *The Anxiety Toolkit: Strategies for Managing Your Anxiety So You Can Get on with Your Life.* New York: Piatkus Books, 2015.

Brantley, Jeffrey. *Calming Your Anxious Mind: How Mindfulness and Compassion Can Free You from Anxiety, Fear, and Panic.* Oakland, CA: New Harbinger Publications, 2007.

Davis, Martha, Elizabeth Robbins Eshelman, and Matthew McKay. *The Relaxation & Stress Reduction Workbook.* Oakland, CA: New Harbinger Publications, 2008.

Gillihan, Seth. *Retrain Your Brain: Cognitive Behavioral Therapy in 7 Weeks — A Workbook for Managing Depression and Anxiety.* Berkeley, CA: Althea Press, 2016.

Kumar, Sameet M. *The Mindful Path Through Worry and Rumination.* Oakland, CA: New Harbinger Publications, 2010.

Leahy, Robert L. *The Worry Cure: Seven Steps to Stop Worry from Stopping You.* New York: Harmony Books, 2005.

SOCIAL ANXIETY DISORDER

Antony, Martin M., and Richard P. Swinson. *The Shyness and Social Anxiety Workbook: Proven Step-by-Step Techniques for Overcoming Your Fear.* Oakland, CA: New Harbinger Publications, 2008.

Butler, Gillian. *Overcoming Social Anxiety and Shyness: A Self-Help Guide Using Cognitive Behavioral Techniques.* New York: Basic Books, 2008.

Fleming, Jan E., and Nancy L. Kocovski. *The Mindfulness and Acceptance Workbook for Social Anxiety and Shyness.* Oakland, CA: New Harbinger Publications, 2013.

Markway, Barbara G., and Gregory P. Markway. *Painfully Shy: How to Overcome Social Anxiety and Reclaim Your Life.* New York: St. Martin's Griffin, 2013.

GENERALIZED ANXIETY DISORDER

Dugas, Michel J., and Melisa Robichaud. *The Generalized Anxiety Disorder Workbook: A Comprehensive CBT Guide for Coping with Uncertainty, Worry, and Fear.* Oakland, CA: New Harbinger Publications, 2015.

PANIC DISORDER AND AGORAPHOBIA

Burns, David D. *When Panic Attacks: The New, Drug-Free Anxiety Therapy That Can Change Your Life.* New York: Morgan Road Books, 2006.

Pollard, C. Alec, and Elke Zuercher-White. *The Agoraphobia Workbook: A Comprehensive Program to End Your Fear of Symptom Attacks.* Oakland, CA: New Harbinger Publications, 2003.

Zuercher-White, Elke. *An End to Panic: Breakthrough Techniques for Overcoming Panic Disorder.* Oakland, CA: New Harbinger Publications, 1998.

SPECIFIC PHOBIAS

Antony, Martin M., and Michelle G. Craske. *Mastering Your Fears and Phobias: Workbook*. New York: Oxford University Press, 2008.

Brown, Duane. *Flying Without Fear*. Oakland, CA: New Harbinger Publications, 2009.

Online

SUPPORT NETWORKS

ADAA.org/supportgroups: The Anxiety and Depression Association of America (ADAA) provides a comprehensive list of community and online support groups for anxiety disorders in the United States, Canada, Mexico, South Africa, and Australia.

Nami.org/find-support: The National Alliance on Mental Illness (NAMI) offers resources for finding support for anxiety disorders.

SocialAnxietySupport.com/groups: The Social Anxiety Support (SAS) website provides a list of social anxiety support groups in the United States, Canada, the United Kingdom, New Zealand, Australia, India, and Ireland.

7cups.com: 7 Cups of Tea is a free online emotional support service with trained listeners who offer support for everyday issues. They also offer an app for most smartphones.

INTERACTIVE PROGRAMS

Ecouch.anu.edu.au: E-couch is a free online program designed to help you develop coping strategies for generalized anxiety disorder and social anxiety disorder.

Moodgym.anu.edu.au: Mood Gym is an interactive online program that teaches the principles of CBT for depression and anxiety.

INFORMATION

ADAA.org: The Anxiety and Depression Association of America (ADAA) provides articles with helpful information on a variety of anxiety topics.

NIMH.nih.gov: The National Institute of Mental Health (NIMH) offers information about each different type of anxiety disorder.

PsychCentral.com: Psych Central is a good resource to learn more about anxiety and recent research.

PsychologyToday.com: Psychology Today offers articles and blog posts written by experts on a variety of anxiety topics.

SocialAnxietyInstitute.org: Founded by Dr. Thomas Richards, the Social Anxiety Institute offers articles and programs for overcoming social anxiety.

Verywell.com: Verywell offers hundreds of articles about each type of anxiety disorder written by experts in the field.

FINDING A THERAPIST

FindCBT.org: The Association for Behavioral and Cognitive Therapies' find-a-CBT-therapist tool.

Locator.apa.org: The American Psychological Association's psychologist locator.

Treatment.adaa.org: The Anxiety and Depression Association of America's find-a-therapist tool.

UCompareHealthCare.com: Search for and compare care based on your location.

RELAXATION

CampusMentalHealth.ca/resource/mcmaster-guided-relaxation-cd: McMaster University in Ontario, Canada, offers a free MP3 version of a guided relaxation CD, including diaphragmatic breathing, progressive muscle relaxation, autogenic training, and guided imagery.

FitnessBlender.com: Fitness Blender offers free full-length workout videos, including those incorporating yoga and relaxation.

Youtube.com/user/yogawithadriene: Yoga with Adriene is an online yoga community with free yoga videos.

Apps

ACT Coach: This app guides you through the concepts of acceptance and commitment therapy and includes mindfulness exercises.

Anxiety Coach: This app designed by the Mayo Clinic is aimed at reducing anxiety, fear, and worry.

CBT-i Coach: This app is designed to help with disruptions in sleep, which may result from anxiety.

Pacifica: This app introduces CBT concepts and teaches deep breathing, progressive muscle relaxation, and mindfulness meditation.

Worry Watch: This app allows you to document your worry, track outcomes, and compare your expectations to outcomes in situations.

Hotlines

National Alliance on Mental Illness (NAMI) HelpLine: 1-800-950-NAMI (6264)

National Suicide Prevention Lifeline: 1-800-273-TALK (8255)

Trevor Project Lifeline: 1-866-488-7386

Trans Lifeline: 1-877-565-8860

REFERENCES

ABC News. "Barbra Streisand Looks Back on 25 Years." September 22, 2005. Accessed June 1, 2017. www.abcnews.go.com/Primetime/Entertainment /story?id=1147020&page=1.

Alden, Alison. "Using Dialectical Behavior Therapy (DBT) to Treat Anxiety Disorders." Accessed June 1, 2017. www.anxietytreatmentcenter .com/2016/12/06/dr-alden-explains-use-dbt-anxiety-treatment/.

American Psychiatric Association. *Diagnostic and Statistical Manual of Mental Disorders* Fifth Edition. Arlington, VA: American Psychiatric Publishing, 2013.

American Psychological Association, Society of Clinical Psychology. "What Is Exposure Therapy?" Accessed June 1, 2017. www.div12.org/sites/default/files /WhatIsExposureTherapy.pdf.

Antony, Martin M., and Richard P. Swinson. *The Shyness and Social Anxiety Workbook: Proven, Step-by-Step Techniques for Overcoming Your Fear.* 2nd ed. Oakland, CA: New Harbinger, 2008.

Anxiety and Depression Association of America. "Complementary and Alternative Treatments." Accessed June 1, 2017. www.adaa.org/finding-help /treatment/complementary-alternative-treatment.

Anxiety and Depression Association of America. "Medication." Accessed June 1, 2017. www.adaa.org/finding-help/treatment/medication.

Anxiety and Depression Association of America. "Therapy." Accessed June 1, 2017. www.adaa.org/finding-help/treatment/therapy.

Bandelow, Borwin, Markus Reitt, Christian Röver, Sophie Michaelis, Yvonne Görlich, and Dirk Wedekind. "Efficacy of Treatments for Anxiety Disorders: A Meta-Analysis." *International Clinical Psychopharmacology* 30, no. 4 (July 2015): 183–92. doi:10.1097/YIC.0000000000000078.

Bandelow, Borwin, and Sophie Michaelis. "Epidemiology of Anxiety Disorders in the 21st Century." *Dialogues in Clinical Neuroscience* 17, no. 3 (September 2015): 327–355. pubmedcentralcanada.ca/pmcc/articles/PMC4610617/.

Beck, Judith S. *Cognitive Behavior Therapy: Basics and Beyond.* 2nd ed. New York: The Guilford Press, 2011.

Benson, Herbert, and Miriam Z. Klipper. *The Relaxation Response.* New York: Harper Collins, 1975.

Bourne, Edmund. *The Anxiety and Phobia Workbook.* 5th ed. Oakland, CA: New Harbinger, 2010.

Boyes, Alice. *The Anxiety Toolkit: Strategies for Managing Your Anxiety So You Can Get on with Your Life.* London, UK: Piatkus, 2015.

Butler, Andrew C., Jason E. Chapman, Evan M. Forman, and Aaron T. Beck. "The Empirical Status of Cognitive-Behavioral Therapy: A Review of Meta-Analyses." *Clinical Psychology Review* 26, no. 1 (January 2006): 17–31. doi:10.1016/j.cpr.2005.07.003.

Canadian Agency for Drugs and Technologies in Health, CADTH Rapid Response Reports. "Neurofeedback and Biofeedback for Mood and Anxiety Disorders: A Review of the Clinical Evidence and Guidelines—an Update." August 26, 2014. Accessed June 1, 2017. www.ncbi.nlm.nih.gov/books/NBK253820/.

Carroll, D., C. Ring, M. Suter, and G. Willemsen. 2000. "The Effects of an Oral Multivitamin Combination with Calcium, Magnesium, and Zinc on Psychological Well-Being in Healthy Young Male Volunteers: A Double-Blind Placebo-Controlled Trial." *Psychopharmacology* 150, no. 2 (June 2000): 220–225. doi:10.1007/s002130000406.

Ciocchi, S., J. Passecker, H. Malagon-Vina, N. Mikus, and T. Klausberger. "Brain Computation. Selective Information Routing by Ventral Hippocampal CA1 Projection Neurons." *Science* (New York) 348, no. 6234 (May 1, 2015): 560–563. doi:10.1126/science.aaa3245.

Crane, Rebecca. *Mindfulness-Based Cognitive Therapy*. New York: Routledge, 2009.

Davis, Martha, Elizabeth Robbins Eshelman, and Matthew McKay. *The Relaxation & Stress Reduction Workbook*. 6th ed. Oakland, CA: New Harbinger, 2008.

Dugas, Michel J., and Melisa Robichaud. *Cognitive-Behavioral Treatment for Generalized Anxiety Disorder: From Science to Practice*. Abingdon, UK: Routledge, 2006.

Estroff Marano, Hara. "Why We Procrastinate: Procrastinators Are Made Not Born. Experts Show Why People Choose Sabotage over Self-Regulation." *Psychology Today*. July 1, 2005. Accessed June 1, 2017. www.psychologytoday.com/articles/200507/why-we-procrastinate.

Golden, William L. "Cognitive Hypnotherapy for Anxiety Disorders." *The American Journal of Clinical Hypnosis* 54, no. 4 (April 2012): 263–274. doi:10.1080/00029157.2011.650333.

Goyal, Madhav, Sonal Singh, Erica M. S. Sibinga, Neda F. Gould, Anastasia Rowland-Seymour, Ritu Sharma, Zackary Berger, et al. "Meditation Programs for Psychological Stress and Well-Being: A Systematic Review and Meta-Analysis." *JAMA Internal Medicine* 174, no. 3 (March 2014): 357–368. doi:10.1001/jamainternmed.2013.13018.

Greeson, Jeffrey, and Jeffrey Brantley. "Mindfulness and Anxiety Disorders: Developing a Wise Relationship with the Inner Experience of Fear." *Clinical Handbook of Mindfulness*, Fabrizio Didonna, editor. New York: Springer, 2008.

Harris, Russell. "Embracing Your Demons: An Overview of Acceptance and Commitment Therapy." *Psychotherapy in Australia* 12, no. 4 (August 2006): 2–7. Accessed June 1, 2017. www.livskompass.se/wp-content/uploads/2012/11/Russ_Harris_A_Non-technical_Overview_of_ACT.2006.pdf.

Harris, Russell. *The Happiness Trap: How to Stop Struggling and Start Living: A Guide to ACT*. Boulder, CO: Trumpeter, 2008.

Harvard Health Publications. "Simple Changes, Big Rewards: A Practical, Easy Guide for Health, Happy Living." Accessed June 1, 2017. www.health.harvard

.edu/mind-and-mood/simple-changes-big-rewards-a-practical-easy-guide
-for-healthy-happy-living.

Hayes, Sarah A., Nathan A. Miller, Debra A. Hope, Richard G. Heimberg, and Harlan R. Juster. "Assessing Client Progress Session by Session in the Treatment of Social Anxiety Disorder: The Social Anxiety Session Change Index." *Cognitive and Behavioral Practice* 15, no. 2 (May 2008): 203–2011. doi:10.1016/j. cbpra.2007.02.010.

Hettema, J. M., M. C. Neale, and K. S. Kendler. "A Review and Meta-Analysis of the Genetic Epidemiology of Anxiety Disorders." *The American Journal of Psychiatry* 158, no. 10 (October 2001): 1568–1578. doi:10.1176/appi.ajp.158.10.1568.

Hood, Heather K., and Martin M. Antony. "Evidence-Based Assessment and Treatment of Specific Phobias in Adults." In *Intensive One-Session Treatment of Specific Phobias*, edited by Thompson E. Davis III, Thomas H. Ollendick, and Lars-Göran Öst. New York: Springer-Verlag, 2012.

Jacobson, Edmund. *Progressive Relaxation: A Physiological and Clinical Investigation of Muscular States and Their Significance in Psychology and Medical Practice.* Chicago: University of Chicago Press, 1938.

Jorm, Anthony F., Helen Christensen, Kathleen M. Griffiths, Ruth A. Parslow, Bryan Rodgers, and Kelly A. Blewitt. "Effectiveness of Complementary and Self-Help Treatments for Anxiety Disorders." *The Medical Journal of Australia* 181, no. 7 (October 4, 2004): S29–46. www.ncbi.nlm.nih.gov/pubmed/15462640.

Kessler, Ronald C., Patricia Berglund, Olga Demler, Robert Jin, Kathleen R. Merikangas, and Ellen E. Walters. "Lifetime Prevalence and Age-of-Onset Distributions of DSM-IV Disorders in the National Comorbidity Survey Replication." *Archives of General Psychiatry* 62, no. 6 (2005): 593–602. doi:10.1001/archpsyc.62.6.593.

Kessler, Ronald C., Wai Tat Chiu, Olga Demler, and Ellen E. Walters. "Prevalence, Severity, and Comorbidity of 12-Month DSM-IV Disorders in the National Comorbidity Survey Replication." *Archives of General Psychiatry* 62, no. 6 (June 2005): 617–627. doi:10.1001/archpsyc.62.6.617.

Leahy, Robert L. *The Worry Cure: Seven Steps to Stop Worry from Stopping You.* New York: Harmony Books, 2005.

Leichsenring, Falk, Wolfgang Hiller, Michael Weissberg, and Eric Leibing. "Cognitive-Behavioral Therapy and Psychodynamic Psychotherapy: Techniques, Efficacy, and Indications." *American Journal of Psychotherapy* 60, no. 3 (2006): 233–259. www.ncbi.nlm.nih.gov/pubmed/17066756.

Manzoni, Gian Mauro, Francesco Pagnini, Gianluca Castelnuovo, and Enrico Molinari. "Relaxation Training for Anxiety: A Ten-Years Systematic Review with Meta-Analysis." *BMC Psychiatry* 8 (June 2008): 41. doi:10.1186/1471-244X-8-41.

Markowitz, John C., Joshua Lipsitz, and Barbara L. Milrod. "Critical Review of Outcome Research on Interpersonal Psychotherapy for Anxiety Disorders." *Depression and Anxiety* 31, no. 4 (April 2014): 316–325. doi:10.1002/da.22238.

Mathews, John. "Stoicism and CBT: Is Therapy a Philosophical Pursuit?" December 6, 2015. Accessed June 1, 2017. www.vacounseling.com/stoicism-cbt/.

Miller, John J., Ken Fletcher, and Jon Kabat-Zinn. "Three-Year Follow-Up and Clinical Implications of a Mindfulness-Based Stress Reduction Intervention in the Treatment of Anxiety Disorders." *General Hospital Psychiatry* 17 (1995): 192–200. doi:10.1016/0163-8343(95)00025-M.

Moscovitch, David A. "What Is the Core Fear in Social Phobia? A New Model to Facilitate Individualized Case Conceptualization and Treatment." *Cognitive and Behavioral Practice* 16, no. 2 (May 2009): 123–134. doi:10.1016/j.cbpra.2008.04.002.

Młyniec, Katarzyna, Claire Linzi Davies, Irene Gómez de Agüero Sánchez, Karolina Pytka, Bogusława Budziszewska, and Gabriel Nowak. "Essential Elements in Depression and Anxiety. Part I." *Pharmacological Reports: PR* 66, no. 4 (2014): 534–544. doi:10.1016/j.pharep.2014.03.001.

National Center for Complementary and Integrative Health. "Relaxation Techniques for Health." Accessed June 1, 2017. www.nccih.nih.gov/health/stress/relaxation.htm.

National Institute of Mental Health. "Anxiety Disorders." Accessed June 1, 2017. www.nimh.nih.gov/health/topics/anxiety-disorders/index.shtml.

National Institute of Mental Health. "Any Anxiety Disorder Among Adults." Accessed June 1, 2017. www.nimh.nih.gov/health/statistics/prevalence /any-anxiety-disorder-among-adults.shtml.

National Institute of Mental Health. "Mental Health Medications." Accessed June 1, 2017. www.nimh.nih.gov/health/topics/mental-health-medications /index.shtml.

National Institute of Mental Health. "Specific Phobias." Accessed June 1, 2017. www.nimh.nih.gov/health/topics/anxiety-disorders/specific-phobias.shtml.

Norton, Alice R., Maree J. Abbott, Melissa M. Norberg, and Caroline Hunt. "A Systematic Review of Mindfulness and Acceptance-Based Treatments for Social Anxiety Disorder." *Journal of Clinical Psychology* 71, no. 4 (2015): 283–301. doi:10.1002/jclp.22144.

Oliveira, Ivaldo Jesus Lima de, Victor Vasconcelos de Souza, Vitor Motta, and Sérgio Leme Da-Silva. "Effects of Oral Vitamin C Supplementation on Anxiety in Students: A Double-Blind, Randomized, Placebo-Controlled Trial." *Pakistan Journal of Biological Sciences: PJBS* 18, no. 1 (2015): 11–18.

Otte, C. "Cognitive Behavioral Therapy in Anxiety Disorders: Current State of the Evidence." *Dialogues in Clinical Neuroscience* 13, no. 4 (December 2011): 413–421. www.ncbi.nlm.nih.gov/pmc/articles/PMC3263389/.

Perry, R., R. Terry, L. K. Watson, and E. Ernst. "Is Lavender an Anxiolytic Drug? A Systematic Review of Randomised Clinical Trials." *Phytomedicine: International Journal of Phytotherapy and Phytopharmacology* 19, no. 8–9 (June 15, 2012): 825–835. doi:10.1016/j.phymed.2012.02.013.

Piccirillo, Marilyn L., M. Taylor Dryman, and Richard G. Heimberg. "Safety Behaviors in Adults with Social Anxiety: Review and Future Directions." *Behavior Therapy* 47, no. 5 (2016): 675–687. doi:10.1016/j.beth.2015.11.005.

Richards, Thomas A. "What You Fear the Most Cannot Happen." *The Anxiety Network*. Accessed June 1, 2017. www.anxietynetwork.com/content/what-you-fear-most-cannot-happen.

Setzer, William N. "Essential Oils and Anxiolytic Aromatherapy." *Natural Product Communications* 4, no. 9 (September 2009): 1305–1316. www.ncbi.nlm.nih.gov/pubmed/19831048.

Sirois, Fuschia M. "Is Procrastination a Vulnerability Factor for Hypertension and Cardiovascular Disease? Testing an Extension of the Procrastination-Health Model." *Journal of Behavioral Medicine* 38, no. 3 (March 2015): 578–589. doi:10.1007/s10865-015-9629-2.

Steimer, Thierry. "The Biology of Fear- and Anxiety-Related Behaviors." *Dialogues in Clinical Neuroscience* 4, no. 3 (September 2002): 231–49.

Takeda, Atsushi, Haruna Tamano, Fumika Kan, Hiromasa Itoh, and Naoto Oku. 2007. "Anxiety-like Behavior of Young Rats after 2-Week Zinc Deprivation." *Behavioural Brain Research* 177, no. 1 (2007): 1–6. doi:10.1016/j.bbr.2006.11.023.

Vanity Fair. "A Star Is Reborn." November 1994. Accessed June 1, 2017. www.barbra-archives.com/bjs_library/90s/vanityfair_94_streisand.html.

Watson, John B. "Psychology as the Behaviorist Views It." *Psychological Review* 20, no. 2 (March 1913): 158–177. doi:10.1037/h0074428.

Wong, Quincy J., Bree Gregory, Jonathan E. Gaston, Ronald M. Rapee, Judith K. Wilson, and Maree J. Abbott. "Development and Validation of the Core Beliefs Questionnaire in a Sample of Individuals with Social Anxiety Disorder." *Journal of Affective Disorders* 207 (January 2017): 121–127. doi:10.1016/j.jad.2016.09.020.

INDEX

ACKNOWLEDGMENTS

It was in the spring of 2015 when I first spoke to editor Nana K. Twumasi about the possibility of writing a book. I did not know it at the time, but it would be two years later before we would have the chance to collaborate. It goes without saying that this book would not have been possible without Nana's guidance and Callisto Media allowing me this opportunity.

I also owe a debt of gratitude to those who influenced my writing and post-secondary education: My grade 7 and 8 teacher Howard Isaacs, who indulged my love of writing by reading my stories to the class, and my high school English teacher Jim Hartley, for making writing fun. Dr. Mark Cole at Western University, for first introducing me to behavior therapy, and my clinical supervisor, the late Dr. David Rennie at York University, for teaching me the basics of person-centered therapy.

I am also grateful for the work experiences that led me to this point. I am thankful for having the unique opportunity to learn about CBT from Dr. Zindel Segal at the Centre for Addiction and Mental Health, which spurred my later interest in this form of treatment. I am also thankful to Dr. Gill Sitarenios at Multi-Health Systems Inc. for his expert guidance on psychological publishing. Finally, I am honored to have spent 10 years working with colleagues from around the world through Verywell.com. I am lucky to be a part of this network of health experts on every imaginable topic.

Of course, I must also thank my family and friends who made it possible for me to take the time to write this book. To my husband, Rob: thank you for your words of encouragement and checking in on my progress. To my children, Morgan and Tyler, ages 8 and 4: thank you for reminding me daily not to take life too seriously. To my brother, Adrian, a fellow author: thank you for the writing advice you've shared over the years. To my parents Bob and Susan: thank you for your unending support and for showing me what it means to be resilient in the face of adversity. To my mother-in-law, Patti:

thank you for being my biggest fan on social media. I am also eternally grateful to other friends and family who supported me from the sidelines: you know who you are.

Finally, to the audience who followed me from About.com to Verywell.com: Knowing that thousands of you read my articles each day continues to inspire me to help and shows me the enormous promise of self-help for anxiety. It was with you in mind that I embarked on this challenge.

ABOUT THE AUTHOR

Arlin Cuncic, MA, is a former researcher, writer, and editor specializing in anxiety. She completed a BA in psychology from Western University in London, Ontario, Canada, and an MA in clinical psychology at York University in Toronto, Canada. She has worked in a variety of settings in Ontario, Canada, including the CBT unit at the Centre for Addiction and Mental Health, Multi-Health Systems Inc., the psychology department at Western University, and the Thames Valley District School Board. She has written about the struggles faced by those with social anxiety disorder and the people in their lives since 2007 for Verywell.com (formerly About.com). She has a keen understanding of their difficulties and a desire to provide information and resources to help them live their best lives. She lives in the small town of Mount Elgin, Ontario, Canada, with her husband and two children.

ABOUT THE FOREWORD AUTHOR

Licensed psychologist **Seth J. Gillihan, PhD**, is a Clinical Assistant Professor of Psychology in the Psychiatry Department at the University of Pennsylvania. He completed his doctorate at the University of Pennsylvania, where he trained in cognitive behavioral therapy (CBT) and the cognitive neuroscience of mood and emotion. Dr. Gillihan has written and lectured nationally and internationally on CBT and how the brain is involved in regulating our moods. He is the author of the book *Retrain Your Brain: Cognitive Behavioral Therapy in 7 Weeks—a Workbook for Managing Depression and Anxiety*. Dr. Gillihan has a clinical practice in Haverford, Pennsylvania, where he specializes in CBT and mindfulness-based interventions for anxiety, depression, and related conditions. He lives in Ardmore, Pennsylvania, with his wife and three children. Learn more about Dr. Gillihan and find more resources at his website: SethGillihan.com.

CPSIA information can be obtained
at www.ICGtesting.com
Printed in the USA
LVHW071241170722
723693LV00007B/156

9 781623 159733